THREE
IRON MINING
TOWNS

Paul Henry Landis

ARNO PRESS
&
The New York Times

NEW YORK • 1970

Reprint Edition 1970 by Arno Press Inc.

Reprinted from a copy in The State Historical Society of Wisconsin Library

LC# 72-112555
ISBN 0-405-02462-2

THE RISE OF URBAN AMERICA
ISBN for complete set 0-405-02430-4

Manufactured in the United States of America

THREE IRON MINING TOWNS

A Study in Cultural Change

By

PAUL H. LANDIS

Associate Professor of Sociology
The State College of Washington

EDWARDS BROTHERS, INC.

ANN ARBOR, MICHIGAN

1938

FOREIGN AGENTS

H. K. LEWIS & CO., LTD.
136 GOWER STREET
LONDON, W.C.1

MARUZEN COMPANY, LTD.
6, TORI-NICHOME NIHONBASHI
P. O. BOX 605 TOKYO CENTRAL
TOKYO, JAPAN

PRINTED IN U.S.A.

Lithoprinted by Edwards Brothers, Inc., Lithoprinters and Publishers
Ann Arbor, Michigan, 1938

PREFACE

The frontier and especially the mining town
has often been made the setting for American fiction,
no doubt primarily because frontier life has color.
Human nature appears in the rough for there is no
time for the embellishments which come to mask it in
more stable environments.

The frontier is no less a suitable subject
for the student of sociology. He, also, is interested in personality and in the social processes that
operate on the frontier where life is less controlled
by long-established custom and by law.

This study is interested in personalities
and in groups as influences in setting social processes in motion and in producing changes in culture.
It is concerned fundamentally with an analysis of
the shifting social interaction patterns which characterize a community as its group composition is
modified during its normal growth to maturity and in
showing how persistent interaction patterns deter-
mine the trend of cultural growth during its life
cycle.

Few industries that establish community life
are more short lived than mining. The short life
cycle offers an unusual opportunity to bring the
historical processes of social and cultural change
of a community within the scope of a special study.
The short span of time involved permits an accurate
observation of the incidence of change; the speed
of development permits observation of the processes
of growth and maturity; the homogeneity of the

economic and industrial base permits an observation
little complicated by a multiplicity of distinct
social classes and social standards. Under such
circumstances one can be fairly sure of what is going on and why. Even though the study deals with a
single area, the processes and relationships re-
vealed no doubt characterize a larger universe.

Acknowledgment is made to the _American
Journal of Sociology_ (University of Chicago Press);
Social Forces (University of North Carolina Press);
and to _Economic Geography_ (Clark University) for
permission to reproduce materials originally published in these journals.

Pullman, Washington
January 2, 1938

TABLE OF CONTENTS

Chapter   Page

P A R T   I

FACTORS IN CULTURE BUILDING

Chapter I[1]

INTRODUCTION

The Mesabi Iron Range and Its Towns

Driving northward in Minnesota some two hundred miles above the Twin Cities, one reaches a wilderness of burned-over stumps, second-growth ever-
greens, tamarack, and underbrush scattered over
rocky hills intervened by swampy valleys or crystal
lakes. An occasional farmhouse suggests the presence of human life. The area bespeaks an age of
timber now past some thirty years, and an agriculture as yet unborn. The charred stumps and deadened
trees indicate the passing of devastating fires. The
highway at a distance of some sixty miles north of
Duluth leads into cities located in the most unsus-
pected places--cities blotted on the rugged surface
features of an iron range.
This iron-bearing district is known as
the Mesabi[2] Range. Some sixty miles inland from the
northwestern end of Lake Superior it extends for a
distance of approximately eighty miles toward the

---

1. This publication is a digest of the observations and conclusions of a doctor's dissertation on Three Mesabi Iron
Range Towns. Substantiating evidence, documentary citations,
and interview summaries are for the most part omitted here
for the sake of brevity. Bound copies of the full manu-
script, including a bibliography of 180 titles, are on file
in the Library of the University of Minnesota and in the Department of Sociology there. For the most part names of
persons are fictitious although each name represents a real
character on the Mesabi Iron Range.

2. "Mesabi" is the spelling accepted by the National Association of Geographers. This is the form used throughout this
work except where the name has another spelling in the
names of railroad companies, etc.

southwest. Here a narrow strip of hills marks the zone of the world's largest iron ore mines, the mines that have fed the manufacturing cities of the lower lake states for a generation, and will continue to feed them for perhaps another generation.

In the lapse of a few years the ore discoveries of the Mesabi shifted the iron and steel trade from the Ohio valley to the Great Lakes, built eight railroads, caused the development of more than twenty flourishing towns, placed on the Great Lakes the largest commercial fleet in the world, and gave America world supremacy in the iron and steel industry.

On the Mesabi cities have sprung up comparable in many respects to those in other areas of American culture. Immigrants have come to these cities from many nations to mine ore, rear families, and become citizens. Three of the most successful municipalities have been chosen for study.

Hibbing has a population of about 16,000 at the present time. She is a village by her own choice, for some thirty-five years ago she might have been incorporated as a city. She is the wealthy village that boasts of a taxable valuation of $93,000,000 and which has for years spent approximately $2,000,000 in tax moneys annually--a village that is self-labeled "The Iron Ore Capital of the World."

Virginia, the "Queen City of the Range," is the second municipality chosen for study. Virginia boasts of 12,000 population now, though at one time she possessed 2000 more. This city has the "world's largest white pine mill" (now idle), and is also the center of valuable mines and fine public works. It has a national reputation for the successful operation of municipal utilities--its heat, electricity, water, and sewerage systems are unrivaled by any American community. Here history is colored with catastrophe, fires at two different periods having almost completely reduced the city to ashes.

Eveleth,   the third city, has a population
of 7500.   It is also a mining town, is the most
foreign in population, and, at the present time, is
more frequently accused of graft than any other
range town.   Eveleth is the "City on the Hill" by
her own designation.   At one time she gained a national reputation for athletics, which led to an
aftermath of lawsuits involving indictments for the
illegal use of city funds.

Hibbing is located at the west end of the
Range; Virginia and Eveleth are some thirty-five
miles eastward in the center of the Range and are
only four miles apart.   All three municipalities,
and most of the Mesabi Range, are in St. Louis County,
Minnesota.

The Virginia town site was originally plat-
ted between Silver and Virginia Lakes, and On September 16, 1892, the first lots were sold.   On December
7 of the same year the first train arrived over the
Duluth Mesabi and Northern, carrying those interested in business and homemaking.

Hibbing had its humble beginning in 1893.
Hibbing and Trimble, partners in exploration, located
the town site in the midst of a great pine forest.
A clearing was begun June 11, and lots were plotted
and sold.

The village of Eveletn was founded in 1893
by two explorers, the most active of the two being
David T. Adams.   He named the town for a timber
cruiser in the district.   "Hank Hookwith came in to
open a saloon.   Archie McComb had a hotel building
(afterwards destroyed by fire), and Jerry Sullivan
had a boarding house on the side of the future
town....."[3]

In such a manner the Mesabi towns that pro-
vide the subject matter for this study were born.
Today they are the chief municipalities of the
Mesabi.

---

3. Van Brunt, Walter, History of Duluth and St. Louis County,
   ch. 22.

Field of Study

The Mesabi Iron Range presents an opportunity for a study of change that is in many respects ideal. The Range was discovered after the development of the modern newspaper, so that during the early history of each town studied, a newspaper was published and consecutive copies for most years have been filed in the library of the State Historical Society.[4] Machine technique, too was well developed, as were modern means of transportation. The demand for iron ore was at its height soon after the discovery of the Range, and the newly-formed United Steel Corporation and other great capitalistic interests bought up most of the important ore reserves. These combined factors have hastened change in the modifiable characteristics of the natural environment and in the rate of development of culture in a way that has scarcely been equalled elsewhere. Wave after wave of settlers came to the Mesabi for the rewards of work--wages, merchandising profits, and professional salaries. This latter situation offers a possibility for studying the effects of the changing complexion of groups on culture. On the Mesabi, then, one has a fast moving panorama of change. The interactions of changing social groups in a rapidly changing environment have combined with a rapid rate of cultural change. The whole drama has been played in forty years.

The exploitation of America's natural resources has led to the establishment of many one-industry towns. Some of these towns have been built by the companies exploiting the natural resource and have been completely controlled by them. In other towns the industrial concern has developed the resource only, leaving the matter of town development entirely to the public that gathered around the infant industry. The Mesabi Iron Range communities

---

4. The Hibbing Sentinel: The Virginia Enterprise: The Eveleth Mining News.

are of the latter type. The iron mining companies
obtained the underground rights only, being interested primarily in iron ore. The surface rights be-
longed to the public and were controlled by them.
The Mesabi towns, which are the subject of this
study, are not, then, company towns. Company towns
ere usually subject to the complete domination and
control of the industry. The Mesabi towns are independent. This must be kept in mind if the vivid
drama of public-mining-company conflict that has
characterized the socio-economic and political patterns of the Mesabi towns is to be fully appreciated.
        The study is an analysis of one of many
phases of American frontier life. It traces a primitive mining settlement through its founding, youth
and maturity. The mining settlement is but one of
many phases of the American frontier, but none the
less possesses many characteristics which are indic-
ative of the patterns of life as they existed a few
years ago in many parts of the nation. The Mesabi
frontier, like most of the frontiers, is now a matter of history and reminiscence, for the community
has reached maturity and is approaching old age.
        This study gives a close-up picture of the
clash of class interests as they have existed in
American industrial experience. It also shows the
American melting pot in ferment, as thousands of
raw immigrants from all the European countries were
moulded, first into the industrial patterns of the
range and then into the social and political com-
pletion of the community.

Assumptions and Hypotheses

        The basic questions to be answered with re-
gard to the nature of cultural change in the mining
town insofar as this study is concerned are:
        1. Does cultural change in the mining town
occur according to some pattern that can be fairly
accurately described?

2. If some pattern of change is present, how is it to be accounted for? If none exists, they why is culture subject to no observable sequences such as are found in other levels of phenomena?

Since it is assumed that cultural dynamics does not necessarily reside in the culture itself, it is legitimate to seek for causes of cultural change outside of culture. We may seek the drive for cultural change in the social group or in its habitat, as well as in the history of the culture.

In accordance with this position the following hypotheses are postulated:

1. Cultural change in the mining town probably occurs according to a pattern that can be observed and described.

2. If the first hypothesis is correct, the forces determining the pattern of change can perhaps be located in culture itself or in these closely related realms of phenomena which are intimately connected with culture--the world of human qualities or of natural conditions.

3. The most fruitful place to seek the forces determining cultural change is in the social group.

More specific statements of hypotheses are made in connection with the data presented in different sections of the study.

The approach in this study is, then, synthetic in the sense that various levels of phenomena are considered as possible sources of energy causing cultural change. Particular attention is given to the bearing of group interaction upon cultural change, although the effects of cultural history, of geographical factors and of biological factors are considered.

Use of Terms

Culture: Civilization. The term is used in its anthropological sense to include both material and non-material traits.

Society: Interacting groups inhabiting a common area. In this case the iron range towns are the area, and the groups are the industrial and labor groups and the public.

Industrial group: Managers and owners of the iron mining industry.

Labor group: Chiefly the laborers in the iron mining industry.

Public: Those who are neither mine laborers nor industrialists, but who, as members of the community, are necessarily concerned in the activities of the other two groups. The public consists largely of professional men, business men, and technicians.

Interaction: A blanket term covering the various processes of inter-group and intra-group intercourse, such as conflict, cooperation, domination, and subordination.

Community, town, municipality: All of these terms are used interchangeably in referring to the towns studied. A rigid distinction between village, town, and city is difficult to follow since two of the municipalities have passed through the first two of these stages and are now cities, while Hibbing has always remained a village even though it is the largest of all Mesabi Range municipalities.

Chapter II

THE GEOGRAPHICAL FACTOR IN RANGE HISTORY

It is difficult to strip a geographical area of its cultural super-structure in order to see it in its purely natural aspects. Once culture building begins, the setting may be radically changed, especially where the culture building group is possessed of technological devices capable of controlling nature to a considerable degree.

A survey of the history of the people who have inhabited the Mesabi indicates that different groups have utilized different natural resources. For instance, one group has sought wild game, another tillable soil, another minerals. The natural environment has been relatively constant for several centuries. Consequently, all present resources have been available to previous groups. Yet, each group has specialized in exploiting a selected resource. This fact merits an explanation.

Resources of the Mesabi

From our present knowledge, it appears that the original resources of the Mesabi Range were: (1) Flora, a virgin forest, principally pine; undergrowth with fruits and berries in great abundance; pin cherries, choke cherries, June berries, raspberries, strawberries, huckleberries, and blueberries; (2) Fauna, moose; bear and deer; many small game animals and furbearing animals; waterfowl and freshwater fish abounding in the lakes; (3) Soil, a fertile and well-watered soil, but rugged and rocky, in places swampy,

10

and everywhere so covered with trees that roots for-
bade tillage until they had been removed; (4) Minerals, vast beds of iron ore that lay near the surface
in loose formation.

Early Uses of the Mesabi

The Mesabi district was the possession of
the Chippewa (Ojibway) Indians until January 1, 1855.
The native tribes lived chiefly by hunting, using
wild game and berries for food. Theirs was a hunting culture. Agriculture as they practiced it was
of the most rudimentary sort. Nor did they make use
of the white pine or the iron ore that has meant so
much to the white man.
Missionaries seeking to Christianize the
Indians, and fur traders seeking pelts were the first
white visitors. They did not come as did later immigrants, to make homes or settlements, or to conquer the environment.
The Range remained without permanent settlements until the development of mining. A gold rush
to the Vermilion Range in 1865 took large numbers
of travelers through the district, but these men
sought gold--they would probably have had no interest
in iron ore even though they had known of its existence.
Lumbering reached its peak on the Mesabi
about 1880 to 1890. The lumbermen saw and sought
only one resource--pine. The land to them had no
other meaning; timber rights were their only concern.
Mineral rights were not considered in acquiring the
land or in disposing of it after it was stripped of
its forests.
Lumbering in the Lake Superior region was
carried forward on a large scale. In the early days
tremendous loads of logs were hauled in these northern forests. Massive sleds loaded with logs trav-
ersed areas in winter over which it was impossible

to travel in summer by any type of vehicle. An early
observer viewing the forests in what is now the Virginia district thought there was timber enough for
hundreds of years, but it was gone in twenty-five or
thirty years. An extensive strip of virgin timber
near Hibbings believed by early explorers to be inexhaustible, was completely gone in fifteen years
after the beginning of the lumbering operations.

      Lumbermen left behind only the ruins of their
exploitation--stumps, underbrush, and burned-over
areas. They did not build a single city of permanence in this forest, not even a permanent dwelling.
With the passing of lumber they, like the "lumber
jacks," migrated to virgin supplies in the West, or
turned to other enterprises in nearby cities. Many
timber barons allowed the land to revert to the State
to avoid taxes, or sold it for what they could get.

Discovery of Mesabi Ore

      Little did the lumbermen know that beneath
the roots of the pine stumps they left behind lay
buried treasures greater than the entire timber
wealth of the nation. Some learned it to their cha-
grin after having disposed of their landholdings for
a pittance; others who held their land because of
inability or indisposition to sell it learned of
its value to their permanent advantage.

      As early as 1850 iron ore had been discov-
ered on the Vermilion Range (some 60 miles north of
the Mesabi), by J. G. Norwood. A geological survey
in 1864 led to the discovery of the Soudan Mine on
the Vermilion Range. As early as 1866 Henry H.
Eames, in quest of gold, located iron ore on the
Mesabi Range. Peter Mitchell verified his discovery
in 1869-1870. Not until 1892 did a railroad reach
this range to inaugurate the shipment of ore.

      Never before in the history of the world had
so rich a bed of ore been located. Moreover, it was

found in a loose form, and very near the surface so
that mining by stripping with the steam shovel was
first employed here. The steam shovel made possible
an output without precedent.

This ore apparently had lain undisturbed for
centuries. It was potentially a resource of all
previous peoples that had inhabited St. Louis County.
It was, however, never made an active factor in any
previous culture. Why did this resource take on
meaning at this time? This question is to be an-
swered only by understanding the impact of a machine
age on natural resources.

The Mesabi in an Iron Age

England led the world in iron production in
the nineteenth century. Extensive ore discoveries
brought America to the place of leadership in the
twentieth century. The most important of these was
the discovery of the Mesabi deposits.

In 1929 the United States produced
72,199,815 metric tons of iron ore. In the same
year France produced 51,028,000 metric tons, Great
Britain 13,427,043 metric tons, and Sweden 11,000,000
metric tons. The leadership of the United States
not only began with the development of the Mesabi
Range but has been maintained by its annual production.

Before 1820 the per capita use of iron in
the United States was 40 pounds. This grew to 175
pounds by 1870, and to 400 pounds by 1900. Whitbeck
and Finch state in their Commercial Geography that
"one corporation in the United States now markets
more iron and steel yearly than all the world used
in any year prior to 1880. But a century ago iron
was a luxury--now it is an 'industrial commonplace.'"
In 1907 twelve hundred pounds of ore were used for
every person in the United States. Iron has become
in a real sense, the measure of civilization in our

age. Steel making peoples now dominate the world,
and leadership among nations depends upon iron resources.
     The iron ranges represent the Industrial
Revolution at the raw-materials-end of the process.
Activities at the mines represent the first process
in steel production. The other end of the process,
that of manufacturing the raw material, may be seen
at Pittsburgh and other cities. The Range is thus
tied up with the commerce and industry of the nation.
     The development of the Minnesota Range was
a step in the westward trend of the iron industry.
     Charcoal was employed in the smelting of
iron until about 1850, when anthracite coal came
into use. This development led to a great increase
in ore production in America, and the industry became centered in the anthracite district of eastern
Pennsylvania. By 1875, the use of bituminous coal
led to a shift of the ore smelting district to western Pennsylvania and the upper Ohio Valley.
     Railroad development during the Civil War
period gave the iron industry a great impetus. Soon
after (1884), the first ore from the Lake Superior
district was shipped. Gradually the ore trade and
ore smelting shifted toward the Lake shores. A
large steel plant was developed as far west as
Duluth and coal for smelting was shipped to the ore,
replacing the usual process of shipping the ore to
the coal.
     The shifting areas of ore production follow
the same general trends as do those for ore smelting.
In 1899 New York state mined 1,247,000 tons of ore,
By 1911 this output was reduced to 1,000,000 due to
the competition of Lake Superior area more than to
exhaustion of supply. In 1890 Pennsylvania led in
the production of ore; by 1911 it held seventh place.
The same year Michigan and Minnesota produced more
than three-fourths of the ore of the United States.
In fact, during that year they produced more ore

than the entire United States had produced in 1889.
The first shipment from Michigan ranges was 1856,
from the Vermilion Range in Minnesota in 1884, and
from the Mesabi in 1892. By 1900 the Mesabi Range
was shipping over one-fourth of the ore of the Lake
Superior district, by 1914 almost one-half, and by
1916 about two-thirds. It has been shipping about
two-thirds of the Lake Superior ore even to the
present time.

The Mesabi Range came to the attention of
the iron men just at the time when inventions for
smelting ore with soft coal had reached the place
where ore could be profitably mined in the lake district. The time of the discovery was, then, fortu-
itous. It solved, to a great extent, the problem of
raw materials for a rapidly expanding industrial
civilization with iron as its basic material culture trait. This industrial need gave meaning to
the previously unutilized ore bodies.

Location in Relation to Industry

The resources of the Mesabi have been of
first importance to contemporary man. Next in importance, probably, has been location with refer-
ence to the heart of American industrial life. We
have seen that industrial life gradually shifted
westward with the development of techniques for
smelting iron by the use of soft coal, until the industry was centered in the bituminous coal regions
of the lower lake states. Ore is bulky and the
transportation costs are important items in determining the value of a deposit. The location of the
Mesabi near the shores of one of the Great Lakes is
of the greatest importance.

Ore has been profitably hauled on the Great
Lakes from the Mesabi Range to Pittsburgh, a distance of approximately one thousand miles. It is
only sixty to eighty miles by rail from the various

mines of the Range to lake ports. From these ports
ore goes to the lower lake ports by boat and is reloaded on trains and sent to the coal districts for
smelting. There is a disadvantage--loading and re-
loading--but such efficient machinery has been developed that this handicap has been largely overcome.
In fact, the ore handling equipment of the Lake
Superior district is known as the most efficient in
the world.

At Duluth the ore is dumped from ore trains
into dock bins, and from the bins into ship holds.
At the lower lake ports it is also automatically -
unloaded and reloaded on the ore trains which carry
it to the iron smelting cities. The railroads are
exceedingly economical since they are used almost
exclusively for ore and can carry the maximum traf-
fic. The loaded trains can coast most of the way
from the Mesabi Range to Duluth.

If it were not for these advantages in the
way of water transportation and efficient handling,
it is doubtful whether the Mesabi ore could be
hauled with profit more than half the distance. The
Mesabi ore no longer competes successfully with
Cuban, Chilian, Newfoundland, Spanish, and Swedish
ores in the eastern cities, but so far these cities
have not been important competitors.

The Utilization of Other
Resources in the Environment

The range cities, recognizing that ore is an
exhaustible resource, have tried to plan for the
utilization of other resources that will make for an
enduring future.

Tourists have in recent years been attracted
to the north country during the summer months.
While this seasonal trade stimulates business, it
cannot assure permanence to the community. The natural resources upon which it depends are also·

exhaustible. Fish and game, scenery and climate,
are the drawing cards. Fish and game conservation
measures have to be enforced increasingly to preserve wild life for the future. Cottages and clear-
ings are already marring the landscapes in some
sections. Climate will, doubtless, always be an attraction in summer months.

Probably the most permanent type of community can be built around agriculture, for the soil if
properly used is inexhaustible. The range towns have
recognized the importance of agriculture and have
for some twenty years tried to encourage its development. Many Finnish families have turned to agriculture during periods of industrial inactivity or
strife, and some have succeeded in making a fair
living from the soil, despite the short growing
season and the ruggedness of the surface features.
One can hardly hope that agriculture will be developed sufficiently to support the towns with their
present populations.

Summary

It is clear that the Mesabi, though its resources now appear to be limited largely to ore,
has, in the past, provided for other types of adjustment. For the Indian it was a hunting ground;
for the lumberman it was a country to exploit and
abandon; for the present generation it is a land
of permanent settlements where man can live by mining ore; for the Finn it is a land where agriculture is possible; for the tourist it is a paradise
of lakes, fish, scenery, and climate--a place where
he can find recreation and rest.

The adjustments made by each group have depended upon its cultural possessions. The various
natural resources of the Mesabi have taken on meaning to resident groups only as their culture patterns have been able to utilize them.

Chapter III

POPULATION IN RELATION TO CULTURAL ADJUSTMENT

It was a select group of people that an-
swered the call to mine ore on the Mesabi. There
has been an element of selection in all subsequent
migrations, but uniqueness in population has tended
to disappear as the cultural adjustment has become
more complete. The population has gradually approached the American norm in its composition and
characteristics.

The Population Perspective

The Range represents an association of con-
glomerate peoples such as is found only in the most
cosmopolitan centers in America. They have gathered
to the Mesabi from forty or more nations over a period of forty years. Wave after wave of immigrants
has come soon to be absorbed into the Range civilization. The daring, the adventuresome, the lonesome
lumberjack, the seasonal immigrant who at first returned annually to his homeland in Europe with his
savings, the gambler, the outcast who wanted to hide
from society, the prostitute, as well as the respectable and the elite--all these have come.[1]
On the other hand, there were men born "to
hustle," men who were foresighted, men who were
first in exploiting the earth's treasures; capitalists and engineers, and the middle class of merchants and professional men. Of such characters

1. See Part III for a description of some of these types.

have been the migrants to this community which of-
fered work for the untrained, the unamericanized,
and the uncultured, as well as for the energetic,
enterprising, and venturesome. They were men who
came to exploit, not to cultivate or to conserve.

Phenomenal Growth of Range Towns

The Range towns were boom towns. Their rapid growth is without precedent in Minnesota history.
In eighteen years Virginia reached the 10,000 population mark, and in twenty-eight years Hibbing
passed the 15,000 population mark. In 1900 Eveleth
bade fare to become the largest town of the Range,
as it then exceeded Hibbing in population; however,
it gradually fell to third place in size. Eveleth
reached her numerical climax in 1910, and Virginia
in 1920. Hibbing grew slightly during the last census period (1920-1930), but the rapid growth of
previous decades has not been duplicated. Virginia
lost over 2000 of her population during the last
census period.

Disproportionate Number of Males

The sex ratio of a community is important
not only from the biological standpoint, as it re-
lates to the maintenance of a normal population increase, but also from the psychological and sociological viewpoints as it affects the mental stabil-
ity of the people and determines the trend of cultural development.

The Range towns originally drew the male
sex, many of them young venturesome men without
worldly possessions. The hazards, uncertainties, and
risks of this pioneer front did not attract women in
any great numbers, and even the men attracted were
heavily sprinkled with the Bohemian type who either
had few family attachments, or who were willing to

sever family ties in the hope of bettering their
position or of acquiring new experiences. Women
came later, when the communities bade fair to be
suitable places for home and children.

Even after the towns had been in existence
two years, the ratio of males to females was five to
one. The original census forms for the 1895 State
Census list fifty-three Virginia women as "demimonde," and three as "prostitutes." Thirteen Hibbing
women were listed as "sports." Many men were also
of questionable character, nineteen being listed as
gamblers in this first census of Virginia.[2]

The lack of civic pride, the prominence of
vice in the field of leisure-time activities, and
the laxity in governmental control, all of which
characterized the Range towns during the first ten
years of their existence, can be better understood
when interpreted in the light of the sex ratio then
existent.

Birth and Death Rates Gradually Approach Normal

Immigration has been an important factor in
the population of the Range towns, not only because
of the numbers added, but also because of the high
reproductive rate of the immigrants. For some twenty-five years the birth rate on the Range was excessive as compared to that of other communities. Gradually with the passing of the years, the immigrant
groups have reached the second generation and birth
rates have declined until they are comparable to
other American Communities.

In the early years death rates, especially
among infants, were very high, but they declined
rapidly after 1910. The high proportion of young
people in the communities, until very recent years,
has made for a low death rate.

2. The original census schedules are on file in the Documents
   Department of the State Historical Society at St. Paul.

Excess of Violent Deaths

The number of violent deaths has been high
on the Range. This is to be expected in a community
predominately masculine, where men face the hazards
of industry. The accident rate in mining is taken
up in another chapter, so it is sufficient to state
that previous to 1910 the accident rate was especially high. A report from the Virginia Enterprise of
April 29, 1904 is suggestive. It reads:

There have been 160 accidental deaths on the Range
during the past year. Of this number, thirty-five lost
their lives in mine disasters, twenty-two died of alcoholism and nine met death by gun-shot wounds. The re-
mainder represents suicides, victims of skull fractures,
men who were crushed in the woods and those who died of
exposure to the cold or were drowned or cremated.

Statistics prepared by Alexander Hamilton, deputy
clerk of the district court, prove interesting in that
they give a fair idea of the number of risks run daily
in the work on the railroad. In the vicini_ of Virginia
there were eight deaths in railroad accidents and eleven
in the mines, one from gun-shot wounds, one from opium
poisoning, one sawmill accident, two deaths from alcoholism, six suicides, one murder and one death from exposure
to the cold.

At Eveleth, alcoholism claimed two, a fractured
skull caused the death of one and a broken neck another.

There were a large number of deaths at Hibbing.
The railroad caused thirteen, the greatest number of
fatalities. Mines stood next with twelve, two of which
were from suffocation. Whiskey came next with eleven
victims.

Suicides

The suicide rate in the Range towns has at
times been excessive as compared to that of the
United States registration area. This was, generally

speaking, truer previous to 1910 than later, although
since that time these towns have had fairly high
rates.

The uneven distribution of the sexes in the
early days very likely had a bearing upon the high
suicide rate. A newspaper account of a 1903 suicide
case is typical of a good many of the early reports
of suicides. After the statement of the subject's
death the account reads:

> Christianson came here from Hibbing about a year
> ago, and for several months was employed as porter by
> Ed Finch. He was discharged on account of dissipation,
> and since that time has been employed at various
> places.
>
> He was intoxicated at a late hour Tuesday night,
> Deputy Coroner Lenest says that death had occured
> about twelve hours before the body was found which
> would time the commission of the deed at about six
> o'clock Wednesday morning. It is supposed that he was
> despondent over his habits and consequent inability to
> secure work.
>
> So far as known he had no relatives in this part
> of the country. The body was removed to Hesberg's
> morgue, from which place the funeral was held.[3]

The suicide rate among single people previous
to 1910 was much higher than that for the married
people, but since that time the suicide rate for the
latter group has increased.

The recent high rate among married men suggests that economic difficulties have been a factor, although the suicides are not grouped in the
months when the mines are most inactive, but are
quite evenly distributed throughout the year. It
is possible, however, that economic factors have had
a bearing, and that a good proportion of the cases
have been among the chronically unemployed.

---

3. The _Daily Virginian_, January 23, 1903.

Immigrant Population

The population of the Range towns is an
amalgamation of many nationalities. The Northern
Europeans, the English, Cornish, Welsh, Austrians,
Irish, Finns, Swedes, and Norwegians came first.
Then came the Italians and other Southern Europeans.

> The babel of more than thirty different alien
> tongues mingles with the roar of mine blasts and the
> crash and clank of machinery. Here side by side work
> Finns, Swedes, Montenegrins, South Italians, English,
> Irish, Bohemians, Frenchmen, Hollanders, Syrians, Bel-
> gians, Croatians, Danes, Russians, Magyars, Bulgarians,
> Germans, Greeks, Scotchmen, Welshmen, Dalmations, Nor-
> wegians and Servians.[4]

The population of Hibbing in 1910 was 50 per
cent native born; the balance was foreign born.
Practically the same ratio obtained in Virginia. By
1920 the ratio was about 65 per cent native to 35
per cent foreign born. Hibbing had 77 per cent native born population in 1930, and 23 per cent foreign born; Virginia, 73.2 per cent and 26.6 per
cent respectively, Eveleth had 70 per cent and 30
per cent respectively.
Data on the total foreign population of
Virginia, with the percentage for each nation, for
the three census years 1910, 1920, and 1930, are
available in the United States Census. The dominance of the Finnish and Swedish elements for each
period is noteworthy. The Norwegians also rank
high. Though the Austrians ranked high in 1910,
they have constituted a small percentage of the
population since that time. "Virginia is more of
an American town than are the other towns," is a
comment frequently heard on the Range, or Virginia
is a 'white' town." Southern European immigrants

---

4. Hodges, L., "Immigrant Life in the Ore Region of Northern
Minnesota," Survey, XXVIII, p. 703.

are not considered white folk by many of the local
residents.

Comparable data are available for Hibbing
for 1920 and 1930. The Finnish element constituted over a fourth of the immigrant population for
both census years; the Swedish element constituted
about 11 per cent. Southern Europeans rank high.
The two leading southern European groups were the
Italians and the Jugoslavians, which together constituted approximately 32 per cent of the foreign
born population in 1920 and 35 per cent of the
foreign born population in 1930.

Although statistics are not available for
Eveleth,[5] it is generally conceded that her population is more predominately South European than that
of either of the other Range towns.

Conclusion

It is clear that though the Range population
has in the past been abnormal in most of the characteristics by which populations can be compared--
numerical increase, age groups, sex ratio, marital
status, birth and death rates, violent deaths, and
nationality composition--by 1940, if recent trends
persist, the population will approximate the American norm in most all respects.

As the culture of the Range has approximat-
ed the culture of other American communities it seems
that the population also has approached the American
norm. Advancing material culture was doubtless a
factor in attracting new residents to the Range,
who in turn effected important social and cultural
changes.

---

5. Under 10,000 population and therefore not analyzed in the
reports of the United States Bureau of the   Census.

P A R T   I I

GROUP ADJUSTMENTS DURING THE HISTORY OF THE RANGE

Chapter IV

THE PIONEER PERIOD

"The country was newly settled by vigorous,
adventurous men." Life centered in a struggle against
nature. There was no time for the petty conflicts of
civilizations characterized by leisure. Class strat-
ification had not developed. The two dominant groups,
capitalists and laborers, worked together to conquer
the rugged hills, to span the swampy flats, to sink
mines, to build railroads, and to establish homes and
cities.

The characteristic spirit of the three infant
Range towns is suggested in the box head which appeared on the front page of each issue of the Iron
Village Sentinel during the year 1894--"Man was born
to Hustle." The frontier presents no other alterna-
tive unless it be to perish.

Hibbing was founded in 1893 by Hibbing and
Trimble. Their portable sawmill converted the virgin
pine into lumber for dwellings. Soon homes were
erected, residents came, a railroad was built,[1] and
business men opened headquarters.[2] During the first
season more than a hundred test-pits were sunk within
a radius of three miles of the town site, and the existence of an abundance of ore was assured.

---

1. The Duluth, Mesabi and Northern railway reached Hibbing,
   Oct. 25, 1893.
2. A compilation of business enterprises at the close of the
   first year showed the following: five saloons, five hotels,
   three grocery stores, two meat markets, three real-estate
   dealers, two contractors, one lumber yard, one hardware
   store, a dry goods store, bank, and a jewelry store.

27

A description of the infant village, Eveleth,
and its surroundings as they existed in 1893 is para-
phrased from an article in the Iron Age:[3] There were
not more than 15 buildings in the place all told and
there was not one stock of goods, wet or dry. Various
new mine pits, a hotel, the paint of which hadn't yet
dried, and a bank whose fixtures hadn't arrived, made
up the town. With such a beginning Eveleth, then
only ten months of age, had shipped between 500,000
and 600,000 tons cf the most excellent ore.

Virginia at the time of its founding, presented a picture of pioneer energy and tenacity. The
town was only well started when a forest fire broke
out in the vicinity. Soon it had reached the edge
of the settlement of wooden buildings and in "forty
minutes after the first shack caught fire" the entire
village lay in ashes. Many left the town; the suicide rate rose rapidly, but the majority remained to
rebuild the town. Reconstruction was begun immediately. A description of the one public building which
housed the services for the religious, recreational,
social, and sensuous needs of the community during
the winter after the fire suggests the character of
life. In it were held all "indoor gatherings, church
services, minstrel shows, dog fights, socials, baccha-
nalian carousals, and gambling events." On the ground
floor next to the sidewalk was the village barber
shop. The central room was a saloon, in the rear were
gambling dens and in the back was the Enterprise office. On the upper floor public meetings were held.
At one end was a platform on trestles of beer kegs.[4]

Economic difficulties soon added to the
troubles of the frontier villages. The panic made
itself felt in 1894. It was difficult therefore for
promoters to borrow the necessary money for the large
investments which had to be made in railroads, clearing, test-pitting, and opening of mines. Moreover,

---

3. See LVI, p. 593.
4. See Van Brunt, Walter, History of Duluth and St. Louis County,
   p. 589.

the large bodies of ore discovered were said to have
actually frightened investors. They feared that the
supply of ore was now so great that the market would
be flooded and the product would become practically
worthless.

The work for which laborers had come to the
Range was not to be found. Idle men walked the
streets of the towns for want of employment. Hibbing sent out this notice through the Sentinel in
April of 1894.

"The laborer who hasn't anything else to do might
just as well keep away from Hibbing. We have enough un-
employed--good and husky men who are ready and more than
willing to work--but the fact is that there are two ap-
plicants for every job, where only one is hired. A man
with a little money can by judicious investments soon
double it in Hibbing. A man without money is likely to
play in hard luck."

In Eveletn, men who had formerly been employed in lumbering and test pitting   at $40.00 per
month and their board could not get a day's work.
The iron business was at its worst.

The Mahoning mine paid $40.00 to $60.00 a
month to its few employees at this time.

After pay day a Mahoning miner was looked up to
with respectful awe in Hibbing, and the less fortunate
ones speculated on whether he would buy a railroad, a
line of steamships or go to Europe for an extended vacation. [5]

Fires threatened each of the towns repeated-
ly during the summer of 1894. The grasshoppers ate
up the gardens and crops. Many residents left for
the Dakota wheatfields or other more favorable local-
ities. A Range editor after having lived in the
midst of these experiences commented in Setpember:

In the presence of forest fires and other calami-
ties without end, it is somewhat difficult to work up

5. The Sentinel, April.

the proper enthusiasm over politics. This has been a
wonderful, fateful, and disastrous year. Every day we
hear of some new horror in the way of railway wrecks,
mine disasters, of holecaust, and we begin to think with
Professor Totten and others who believe in the Visible
signs that the end of the weary old world is not far
off.[6]

The darkness of this period, however, soon disappeared. By midwinter lumber camps had taken up all
surplus labor to harvest the timber deadened by the
forest fires. The "lumber jacks" were paid only
$6.00 to $12.00 per month, but at least they were
given work. But by the middle of 1895 the depression was forgotten and each of the towns was being
built rapidly, and the spirit of optimism was in
evidence everywhere.

Buildings were being erected in Hibbing at
the rate of three new structures a week. The hotels
were crowded nightly with newcomers. Population increased at the rate of 100 per week. While sinking
the city well, ore was struck, indicating that the
entire city was underlaid with a rich bed of ore.

Virginia also boomed. "We have seen," said
the editor of the Enterprise, "Virginia grow from an
insignificant crossroad neighborhood to a population
of five thousand in as many months; we have seen it
left as a barren and desolate waste of fire's de-
structiveness and have seen it rebuilt and again
become the only town on the range, as the result of
the united and determined efforts of its enterprising citizens. We shall also see it become the
first city, the only city and the distributing point
for nearly or quite all the business of the entire
range."[7]

Eveleth did not share fully in the prosperity of the nineties. People did not believe there

---

6. Ibid., Sept. 1.
7. Feb. 8, 1895, p. 4.

was much ore in the vicinity. "I had some disap-
pointments," comments its founder, "with my early
townsite enterprise. The influence of so many non-
believers in the existence of ore in the southern
part of township 56, section 17 had its effect--
when I plotted your now beautiful city Eveleth.[8]

The fact was, Eveleth had been plotted over
the best ore deposit in the district. Important
developments did not take place until 1900 when the
town was moved one-fourth of a mile uphill to per-
mit the opening of the Fayal mine.

It appeared, by 1900, that pioneer difficulties were over, but this did not prove to be the
case for Virginia. On June 7 of that year a fire
broke out in one of the new mills and destroyed
nearly all of the business section. Many people
left, but others stayed to rebuild the city.

"The rapidity with which Virginia is rebuild-
ing," said the editor of the Enterprise, "after its
second disaster is a matter of much surprise to visitors to the city. With the new walks laid and the
buildings completed and occupied which are now in
course of construction, the new Virginia will present the handsomest most substantial town of the
Ranges thirty days hence."[9]

This prophecy was literally true. On the
first anniversary of their fire he was able to
write.

Where but one year ago were the smouldering ruins
of the second Virginia, today stands the only brick city
of northern Minnesota. Practically all the burned buildings having been replaced with handsome brick structures,
filled with finer stores and happier homes, as a result
of the well-placed confidence in our future.[10]

---

8. Van Brunt, Walter, op. cit., ch. 22.
9. The Virginia Enterprise, Sept. 14, 1900.
10. Ibid., June 7, 1901.

The newspapers previous to 1900 depict
struggling mining villages on the Mesabi with life
full of irregularities. Numerous accounts of suicides, fights and drunken brawls, deaths from exposure of homeless men in drunken stupors, accidents among laborers in the mines and woods, reports
of criminals being captured who had fled from other
cities to the Range mining centers to lose their
identity among pioneers, cases of the passing of
counterfeit money, printing and forging mining and
lumber company checks, jumping rooming-house board
bills and hotel bills, the operating of "blind pigs"
to avoid paying the liquor license--all these appear
as news items.

Hibbing was so accustomed to the sensational,
that in a week of 1899 when things had been rather
"dead" the press reported, "There are no deaths,
births, marriages, mining accidents, suicides, run-
aways, fires, elopements, stabbing affrays, or
scandal reports this week."

During this early period there was no serious conflict between the industrial group and labor
or the public. The mining industry was considered
the foundation of life in the area and company
rights were seldom challenged. The people having
come to a mining settlement, they expected nothing
better. Even when the strike of 1894 was brought
about by agitators who had come into.the range from
other mining centers, little local cooperation was
obtained from the miners. Moreover, the business
men in the towns threatened to withhold credit from
the strikers if they continued to oppose the mining
companies. These friendly relations toward the
mining companies were maintained until about 1910.

The Transition from Pioneer Society

Soon after 1900 the three towns were assured a permanent existence. The following decade
was characterized by a gradual transition   from

pioneer to permanent society. The non-mining public
increased in the population. This group, being a
normal one composed of married men with wives and
children, demanded conveniences and respectability
of the community in which it lived. This group
fought against the vulgar elements in community
life, and eventually succeeded in bringing about
the eradications of pioneer vices and in increasing
local conveniences.

        During this transition Virginia presents
the most intense struggle for reform in morals.[11]
As early as 1895, a Finnish Temperance Union was
organized. Steps were taken by the city to close
houses of prostitution, gambling dens, and to remove slot machines. By 1902 dice and cards were
specifically banned. Of course, it was impossible
to enforce the laws entirely, but their enactment
gave evidence that the moral development of the town
was a matter of concern with a small public.

        Moral reform got into politics around 1906.
The struggle of parties sponsoring or condemning
vice characterized every political battle for the
following eight years. Some elections were won by
the vice crusaders; others by candidates favoring a
"wide open" policy.

        Hibbing, like Virginia wrestled with the
problem of pioneer vice. Prostitution had been
pretty well obliterated there by 1906 through the
enactment of a statute which banned brothels from the
village. Gambling, however, was a recurrent evil.

        The town boasted of sixty-five saloons in
1909. The editor of the Ore suggested that these
should be cut to about twenty-five and made to pay
a license fee of $1500 to $2000.

        Here an element not found in the other towns,
was injected into the saloon situation. For a
long period there was considerable discussion as

---

11. The history of the political struggle presented here is
    based on news items taken from the bound files of the
    Virginia Enterprise.

to whether Hibbing was in the territory in which
saloons were prohibited by an early Federal treaty
with the Indians. From time to time between the
years 1905 and 1915 saloons were closed and reop-
ened by special acts of the State and Federal courts.
After one such closing of a few days duration, it
was reported that twelve carloads of beer were
shipped in to relieve "the dry spell."[12]

   After the Indian treaty had failed to ban-
ish liquor from the town in 1911 a vote was taken
on the matter, which resulted in 1,160 votes for
licensed liquor, and 295 votes against it. The total village receipts for the year amounted to
$327,238.80 of which $32,150 was from liquor li-
censes. This may have been a factor in swinging
the vote.

   Moral reforms came late in Eveleth. A civic
league was organized in 1905 with a membership of
700. Its purpose was to secure law-enforcement--
especially anti-saloon and health regulations. The
number of saloons was limited to one for every five
hundred people, and all were to be closed at eleven
every evening and all day on Sunday. Crusades
against slot machines and the location of the red-
light district were initiated by the league with
the result that slot machines were banished. The
red-light district was finally segregated and later
driven out of the city, but not until several years
after it had been outlawed in Hibbing and Virginia.

   All in all, respectability was costly in the
mining towns. With the development of standards of
respectability came the accumulation of desires for
comforts and luxuries. These same groups that demanded respectable morals, turned next to exploit
the mining companies through taxation to gain recognition in material culture. They sought privileges and luxuries for themselves, their children,
and for the worker.

---

12. The Sentinel.

In 1908 the newly-elected president of the
Virginia Commercial Club, a recent comer to the
Range, called attention to the fact that the city
then had between nine and ten thousand residents,
yet had no public parks, no playgrounds, few trees,
few lawns, and no flower gardens. He urged cooperation to the end that the citizens might see their
city develop through an increase in public improvements.

Soon Hibbing also was to adopt a new municipal policy. The conservative president of the
village, Dr. Ray, was to be replaced by a man of the
people, Victor Seabold, who was to transform the
village which had been suggestively described as a
"cross between a rat hole and a mud hole" into what
was claimed to be the most wealthy, most lavish,
and most famous village in the world.

Eveleth likewise, even sooner than the other
towns, shook off the crude municipal properties of
her youth and set the pace for the Range in public
works and luxuries.

The development of the desire for conveniences, services, and respectability proved to be
cumulative in nature, and soon led the communities
into conflict with the industrial tax paying group.

These new desires on the part of the public
were destined to disrupt the friendly relations existing between mining company and community; reform
groups and political classes within the public became integrated against the common foe, absentee
capitalists. Thus, the conflict interaction pattern
came to characterize the second period in the history of the mining towns.

This period in Range history is covered in
the next chapter.

Chapter V

THE PERIOD OF CONFLICT

The second period in these mining communities was characterized principally by a struggle between the mining companies and the local public for possession of a share of the economic benefits attainable from the mining of iron ore. Labor took a position with the public so need not be considered separately. The industrial group consisted of the corporations developing the natural resources. The public was composed of the residents of the cities who found expression and unity of action in governmental organization. In the struggle between these groups the corporations sought profits. Political groups, representing the public, desired taxes to be converted into public works' and services by which the community might be enriched.

A summary account of the struggle between the industrial group and the public is presented in this chapter. It seemed best to confine the picture largely to Hibbing. This permits a more detailed description than would be practicable should the struggle in the three towns be thoroughly reviewed. Moreover, Hibbing represents the conflict pattern most clearly, for there the conflict has been overt and may, therefore, be observed readily.

Suffice it to say, however, the conflict pattern has been present in Eveleth in a very overt form and especially so during the last fifteen years. In Virginia the conflict has been much more subtle. In fact, Virginia has not represented, in some respects, the typical mining-town culture, probably due to the fact that she has depended on other industries than mining, notably lumbering.

Hibbing Defies the Mining Companies[1]

The conflict between the mining companies
and the public gathered momentum years before it
broke into an open struggle. The integration established during the hazardous periods of the founding
of the communities disappeared very slowly.

The people in Hibbing elected Dr. H. R. Ray
to the village presidency for six successive terms
previous to the overt expression of the conflict.
Dr. Ray cooperated with the mining companies and
carried out a conservative program as far as public
developments were concerned. Because of his connection with the hospital, where mining companies carried contracts for health service for their men, Dr.
Ray was naturally interested in maintaining friendly
relationships with the mining companies. The towns-
people were led to feel that they owed their existence to the mining companies, and must, therefore,
keep their good will.

During the last year of President Ray's administration, however, sentiment against him began
to accumulate, preparing the way for a new administration.[2] Victor L. Seabold, an attorney and prom-
inent citizen, seems to have been the leader in
condemning the mayor and council for their backward-
ness in city development.

Mr. Seabold later ran for the presidency
and carried the election of 1913. His election
ushered in a new regime for Iron Village. He was
reelected nine consecutive one-year terms. During

---

1. This story of the Hibbing mining company conflict is constructed from news items taken from the bound files of the
   Hibbing Daily Tribune. For a brief summary of the conflict
   for the years 1912 to 1920 see the historical edition of
   this same paper published Dec. 31, 1921. See also Howard,
   A. S., Hibbing, The Old and The New. 1920.
2. See the Hibbing Tribune, Mar. 30, 1915.

this long administration he was never seriously
challenged in an election.

A program for elaborate municipal expenditures was planned under Mr. Seabold's leadership,
and for ten years the city spent money in a high-
handed manner, defying the mining companies and the
law. Seabold proved capable of meeting every attack
of the mining interests and won almost every city-
mining company legal encounter during his long administration. Under Seabold's leadership the village gained a national reputation for public works.

Backing their new mayor, the commercial
club decided in 1913 that the best way to get trade
by the newly completed interurban line and to bring
people to Hibbing was to make the village the most
beautiful one on the Range. The following day the
City Council planned for a great deal of additional
paving and lighting.

However, the Lake Superior Tax Association
was formed during the same year by thirty-one mining companies. Its aim was to secure more reasonable expenditures for municipal improvements. The
association affirmed a friendly attitude toward the
villages, but was interested in getting improvements
economically.

Overt conflict between the village and the
mining companies originated in damage suits brought
about because the mining companies blasted too near
the residential districts of the town. Seabold had
been the lawyer in these original suits, and attained enough recognition as a result of victories
to carry the village election.

The newspaper historians claim that the
blasting had greatly retarded development of the
town. The streets could not be properly lighted
for fear that the blasts would destroy the lamps.
The streets and sidewalks were not paved because
the mining companies might some day take over the
entire village and convert it into a mine pit.

The village had heretofore remained in sub-
jection to the mining companies, as many citizens

felt that the companies were their greatest bene-
factors because they provided for their very existence. They also held that if an attack were made
upon the mine operators they would stop operations
in the district and concentrate their efforts in
other districts, thus leaving the people without
employment. Victor L. Seabold took the opposite position. He announced that the people were less dependent on the mining companies than the companies
were upon the people, and further said that in case
the mines were shut down in the Hibbing district,
he would simply assess the maximum tax upon the
company properties, and start enough public works
in the village to keep all idle men employed. Later,
when the occasion came, the mayor enforced this
threat to the letter. The mining companies stopped
operations in the immediate vicinity for a season,
and during this period there were almost as many men
on the village pay roll as there were voters.[3]

     In retaliation the mining companies refused
to pay their taxes for the latter half of the year
1913. Seabold made various attempts to secure legislation that would compel them to pay; he also
tried to get the Governor to seize their ore stock-
piles. The companies fought back by getting injunctions passed which hindered municipal building
projects temporarily. They were not, however, successful in checking expenditures for any great
length of time.

     In November, 1913, the **News** reported that
Hibbing lived up to its reputation of a million
dollar village by employing expert advice at a cost
of $12,250. This advice uncovered laws that led
to the redemption of $13,000 from the township, due
Hibbing for certain annexations. During the same
year the city spent $41,181.09 on parks, boulevards,
and other city improvements.

     The mining companies made a bold stroke in
the Harrison Bill which was introduced into the

3. See ch. X.

legislature to limit municipal expenditures to 50
per capita. A delegation from Hibbing and from the
other towns attended the hearing at St. Paul, and by
a heroic effort Seabold succeeded in getting the
measure defeated. He returned to Hibbing, where he
was banqueted and treated as a hero. He was known
thereafter as the Napoleon of Hibbing.

The conflict between the village and mining
companies again came to the surface in 1917, when
the mining companies instituted an injunction restraining the village from paying certain bills.

Following this injunction, the mayor and
councilmen were tried for graft, having been charged
with the presentation of fraudulent claims. The
first two officials tried were declared not guilty,
so the other indictments were dropped without trial.
The Hibbing press commented upon the trial as an
attempt on the part of the Steel Company to "railroad" Hibbing officials to prison. Seabold was given
credit for the victory over the Steel Company.

Another angle of the conflict came to focus
in the moving of Hibbing.

The actual moving of the village came, for
the most part, during the years 1918 to 1920, after
the remodeling of streets, lighting, and public
buildings had been completed. The moving was described in the local press as the most gigantic operation of its kind that had ever taken place anywhere.

The occasion, cost, and method of moving
the city is well described in the Historical Edition
of the Hibbing Daily News and Mesaba Ore of October,
1921. The mines had so encroached upon three sides
of the town that the business district was left on
a peninsula surrounded by mines. The problem was
to obtain a new place for the people to live and for
the business establishments to operate. The Iron
Mining Company purchased eighty acres south of the
original town, and moved their employees' homes to
the new site. They allowed the merchants to choose

their sites in New Hibbing. The company then built
three modern business blocks and sold them to the
merchants, helping them to finance the purchase.
The cost of the project of moving is estimated at
$16,000,000.

In old Hibbing, the Seabold administration
had built a city with pavements, white ways, sidewalks, water and sewer systems, and public buildings.
These utilities were scarcely completed when they
were destroyed. The mining companies wanted the ore
under the city and, of course, were expected to pay
again (they had already paid most of the cost of
the improvements through taxation) for all village
property that was to be destroyed. There is considerable evidence that Seabold did not go into the
matter blindly. He, and all other residents of
Hibbing, knew that in the not distant future the
town was to be moved. Apparently this was a matter
for mining companies to worry about.

But the victory was not entirely one-sided.
The moving enterprise had far-reaching implications
for Hibbing. The mining companies purchased only a
part of the town area. Two-thirds of the old townsite was not purchased, so stands today on the
brink of the world's largest iron mine. Property
values have been greatly deflated. Business has
been ruined for the only approach to the city leads
through the new and better Hibbing, a mile south.
The village has, since the move, been divided both
in spirit and in physical autonomy. Seabold lives
in the memory of many as the man who "sold out" his
village.

Hibbing Submits to the Mining Companies

When one studies the trend of events since
1925, it becomes increasingly evident that the position of the combatants is being reversed. The mining companies are becoming the dictators of the

policies which the village must pursue. The mining
companies' victory was won in the reduction of village expenditures through legislative restriction.
The per capita limitation law became effective in
1921, and was modified to further reduce expenditures in 1929.[4]

Village administrations have since found it
well nigh impossible to keep expenditures within
the limits of the per capita law, but when they
have attempted to exceed these limits they have
been threatened with injunctions by the Lake Superior Tax Association, a mining-company organization.

When townsmen in Hibbing saw that they were
defeated by the mining companies, they floated a
$2,000,000 bond issue to cover a part of the indebt-
edness. The total indebtedness of the village in
1921 was approximately $6,000,000.

The conflict with the mining companies, carried on by Mayor Moss for the village since the
moving of Hibbing, has centered in an attempt to
obtain damages for property holders and business men
in the Southern and Pillsbury additions in old
Hibbing. Attempts have been made annually under
one claim or another by organized groups of citizens to receive damages for lost property values
from the mining companies through judicial decision
or through legislation, but all in vain. The matter was even carried to the United States Supreme
Court in 1927. This struggle makes an interesting
story as it has been reconstructed from newspaper
files, but one which is too long to recapitulate
here. The significant point is that Hibbing has
lost the fight. It is learning to bow, even though
unwillingly, to the mining companies.

---

4. See ch. XI.

Eveleth Buys a Reputation
Through Athletic Achievements

The overt conflict due to extravagance in
Eveleth took a rather peculiar turn. It came later
than in Hibbing, reaching its climax in 1923.
Eveleth set out to achieve athletic supremacy at
city expense. The pattern was not new on the Mesabi.
It had been customary for the towns from early days
to buy baseball talent in order that they might be
able to show up well in the league games. Beginning around 1912, the athletic program was broad-
ened in all the Range municipalities. The towns
took on extensive recreational programs sponsoring
winter sports, carnivals, hockey, and curling.
These programs reached their climax in the building
of elaborate recreational buildings in memory of
the World War heroes.

Perhaps the outstanding stroke in attracting
athletic talent to Eveleth was the hiring of Bob
Taylor, World's champion curler, who since his coming has won twelve state championships for the city.

A man by the name of Pratt introduced curling on the Range. For some reason the game took
hold of public interest rapidly. Soon all of the
Range towns had teams and had constructed large indoor playing spaces. Eveleth built the recreational building primarily for the curling club, and put
Bob Taylor in charge of the building as a city employee. By this means she supported the world's
champion curler and developed a whole generation of
curlers, for Taylor not only has cared for the
building but has also taught the game.

Another big stroke in athletic advancement
was effected through the bringing together of a
professional hockey team. Most of the men com-
prising this team were imported from Canada, and

5. This account is based largely on news items found in the
bound volumes of the Eveleth News.

were supported in the city for their prowess in the
game. This team gained a reputation for the town.
It played in the national championship finale los-
ing only to Cleveland, Ohio. Of even more significance was the fact that in 1928, Eveleth was asked
to furnish a hockey team to represent the United
States at the Olympic Games at Amsterdam, Holland.
     The material side of the hockey complex
found expression in the building of a giant hippodrome, which was alleged to have been the largest
indoor rink in the world. After this building was
abandoned the sport was carried on in the recreation
building.
     The building of athletic space and the sup-
port of players, as well as the expense of the
games, required large amounts of municipal funds.
It was the problem of recreational expenditures
that lead to litigation and overt conflict.
     Harry Purim, a local resident, brought
charges against the city officials for having spent
money illegally in building the hippodrome. Purim
was a mining-company sympathizer, his father having
once owned a mine. Local informants suggested to
the writer that Purim was also incited by mining
companies. At any rate, he pushed the suit against
the city officials and in 1923 secured their con-
viction.
     Some $64,000 in obligations to a lumber
company for materials used in the building of the
large hockey rink, to a hotel for the care of vis-
iting athletics and their wives, and for other general promotion expenses were charged to the account
of the city officers on the ground that they had
illegally expended this amount of public funds for
sports.
     Other questionable actions of city offi-
cials, discovered by Garfield Brown, State Public
Examiner, resulted in 1923 in the removal from office of Mayor Camack and councilman Van Kuzkirk by
Governor Preus. Eveleth and the Range revolted

against this action by the Governor, maintaining
that since the city was under a home-rule charter,
the Governor could not remove officers without legal
proceedings. The city officials remained in office,
and the following November they were reelected by a
big majority. The community accepted them as "mar-
tyrs to the cause of the local community," for they
were leaders in the fight against the millionaire
capitalists of the East.

This was only the beginning of difficulties.
Repeated accusations of graft have been brought
against various councilmen and Mayor Camack. These
officers have been indicted by grand juries, but only one councilman has been convicted. He was sent
to prison. The same administration that has been
accused of the most graft was still in office in
1935.

Repeated injunctions against the cities
spending more than the per capita limit have been
instituted by the mining companies. As a result
the city has operated by issuing warrants against
the following year's budget. In 1930 the city
failed to pay the proportion of back debt required
by the per capita law, so the mining companies were
instrumental in imposing an injunction limiting expenditures to $30,000 per month until a stated per-
centage of the outstanding indebtedness was paid.
City affairs are still being conducted in a high-
handed manner, but Eveleth too is bowing to the
mining companies.

Virginia Capitalized Prosperity

Virginia has not been accused of extravagance as the other Range towns have. She has built
extensively and expensively, but has gotten dollar
for dollar value for her citizens from her public
works. Even the mining companies have not objected
strenuously to expenditures of this nature. During

the period when Eveleth was squandering money in
municipal recreation, and Hibbing by the paternalistic policy of employing needless labor and the
careless use of funds in public office, Virginia
was developing her municipal ownership program add-
ing a municipal gas plant, the first on the Range,
and extending city heat to practically the entire
city.

Money vas laid aside for public building
projects, with the result that in 1924 a beautiful
recreational building and city hall were completed
on a strictly cash basis. Virginia built conserva-
tively and has never spent more than $40.00 per
capita,⁶ so is unaffected by the per capita limitation law.

In Virginia the conflict has been primarily
between political groups and not between the public
and industry, though there is a subtle conflict,
which has never appeared on the surface, existing in
this relation.

---

6. Estimate made by City Clerk, Ford, of Virginia in an interview.

Chapter VI

THE PERIOD OF STRUGGLE FOR SURVIVAL

This third period in the history of these
mining towns will undoubtedly be characterized by
abandonment and cultural decay. Industrialists will
remove their enterprises and laborers will leave the
scene when the basic resource can no longer be mined
profitably. The non-mining public will be left behind. Members of this group will have vested interests in the continuation of the society. Their
homes, fortunes, and emotional attachments will be
tied up in the local community. An intra-group
struggle will probably ensue and ultimately deter-
mine those who can survive in the old setting.

This final period will be similar to the
first period in one respect. Society will be characterized by a struggle with nature for maintenance.
However, it will not be labor and industry struggling together to make a resource available as in
the first case, but it will be an intra-group conflict within the public. Again, it will not be a
struggle to develop an abundant resource already
known to exist as in the first case, but it will be
an effort to develop resources that are in themselves neither attractive nor inviting.

The Mesabi has not entirely reached this
stage as yet, so most of the generalizations regarding this period are more in the realm of prediction
than in that of history.

In speculating on the final phase of the
life cycle of mining-town culture, two lines of evidence are followed. The first is found in the adjustment measures employed by the towns in times of

industrial depression when labor could not be depended upon for business and trade. At such times
two types of adjustment have been attempted--the development of an agricultural hinterland and the attraction of a tourist trade. In each adjustment
the public has taken the initiative. As the exhaustion of the ore approaches undoubtedly attempts to
develop these two activities will be intensified by
the town merchants.

A second line of evidence is found in the
adjustments which towns that have been partially
abandoned have made. The only important example on
the Mesabi is Gilbert, which is discussed later. It
presents significant adjustments that are suggestive
of the final period in the history of the mining
town.

Just when the Mesabi will reach the final
period one cannot accurately foretell, but it is a
certainty that its days are numbered.

Let us turn our attention now to a study of
attempts at adjustment that give some hint regarding
the possible future activities of the Range town
public.

Building a Trade Hinterland

The Range municipalities have made concerted
efforts to develop agriculture in the surrounding
hinterland for some twenty years or more, realizing
that in times of industrial depression, and in case
of the future depletion of iron ore, their hope for
survival lay in more permanent industries.

Economic conditions of the winter of 1912
stimulated an intense interest in agricultural developments among business men of the Range. An address
given before the Hibbing Commercial Club at that
time suggests the prevailing conditions and developing sentiment for agriculture. It reads in part:

I do not believe that Hibbing will ever again see
the prosperous times that made us the most talked of town
in Minnesota several years ago. Then there were drills
working all over the iron fields in this section employing skilled labor at high wages and unskilled labor at
much better figures than was the run elsewhere. Stripping operations were everywhere busy and exploration
work of all kinds was going on. Contrast that condition
with the one of today. There remains to be done little
exploration work in this vicinity. Where there were a
hundred drills working here a few years ago there are
not a half dozen now. The open pit mines here are nothing more or less than huge stock piles. There is enough
ore bared to keep the steam shovels busy for years, and
the stripping operations in this section are not to be so
large an item hereafter as in the past. New ranges are
developed and the mining industry in the future, so far
as it affects Hibbing, will be governed largely by the
steel market. Sometimes it will be busy and again it will
be dull. This has never since its inception been a city
of homes in the strictest sense of the term, but it is becoming more so. The man who is interested in Hibbing in
a business way and who intends to live here does not have
to go far into this matter to find that what we need is
more farmers...[1]

    This sentiment has **grown** yearly with recur-
rent industrial depressions and unemployment.
Farmer's fairs held annually in each town, the St.
Louis County Fair, held at Hibbing, booster campaigns, advertising campaigns, carried out under the
supervision of the commercial clubs, potato warehouses for the storage of crops, creameries, special
potato trains exhibiting Range products, and other
devices have been used to stimulate interest. The
merchants rather than the farmers have backed all
propaganda for agricultural developments.
    Each town has tried to cater to rural inter-
ests and rural trade. For instance, Eveleth carried

1. Hibbing **News**. March 1, 1912.

the slogan on a recently issued Commercial Club
folder, "Eveleth--where agriculture and mining meet."
The Eveleth News published a special farmer's day
historical edition, September, 1922, describing farming in the hinterland and extolling the developmental
possibilities of farming and dairying. The Virginia
Queen City Sun carried the following box heads during the summer of 1932. "A wild acre of land is a
liability to the State and to this community. A
cleared acre of land is an asset. Encourage the
farmer to clear his land."

Virginia merchants seem to have a particular
awareness of the importance of capitalizing their
trade possibilities. This is suggested in the comments of the merchants as one discusses the future
with them.

The comments of the business men are more
optimistic with regard to agricultural developments
than past trends justify. There has been very little increase in rural population for years in St.
Louis County. The strike of 1907, in which the
Finnish anarchist group took the leading part, drove
thousands of Finnish miners to the soil. During
this strike the mining companies imported Southern
Europeans as strike breakers, and for several years
after the strike they discriminated against Finns
in selecting employees. The increase in rural population from 20,531 in 1900 to 47,211 in 1910 is
explained to a considerable extent by this situation. Since 1910 there has been comparatively little increase in rural population in the county. Between 1910 and 1920 there was an increase of 7.8
per cent, but between 1920 and 1930 there was a
decrease of 4.9 per cent.

The rigorous climatic conditions of St.
Louis County, the rocky soil, and the almost uncon-
querable underbrush make one wonder if any peoples
other than sturdy European peasants, who have never
known anything but hardships and poverty, would possess the patience necessary to wrest a living from
most areas in the County.

Baiting a Tourist Trade

A second enterprise which the Range towns
have encouraged, chiefly through commercial club
propaganda, is the advertising of the hinterland as
a summer vacation center of unusual attractions.

The three Range towns are in the heart of
the great "Arrowhead District," the so-called
"Playground of the Nation." Virginia and Eveleth
are on roads leading to the various Lakes and resorts: Eveleth is the first city the tourist
strikes on his trip north from Duluth, the "Tourists'
Gateway to the Mines and Lakes Country." Hibbing
is on the highway that leads into the arrowhead
district from the southwest. More than 5000 tourists pass through the Mesabi Iron Range towns annually.

The Range towns raised $30,000 in the fall
of 1926 with which to advertise the Arrowhead District. Each of the towns has circulated attractive
folders since 1930, baiting tourists with pictures
of lakes, fish, golf courses, scenery, iron mines,
magnificent public buildings, and swimming beaches.

There is good reason to believe that as
mining declines at some future time, tourist patronage will be sought increasingly.

The Leach Town

Gilbert is located in the center of important ore reserves, but reserves on which the mining
companies hold long time leases. Years ago, after
the mining location had grown to a prosperous city
of some 3500 population, the mining companies left
the field to work deposits on which they held short
time leases. This meant the complete abandonment of
mining activities for several years; labor left the
city. Ore bodies are taxable even when they are not
being mined, so iron ore taxes were still available

to the public. When the mines closed, many of those
business men who kept their places open turned to
vice for maintenance, and an abnormally large number
of the rest of the public turned to city and school
employment made possible by ore tax revenues.

During the days of national prohibition the
combined saloons and brothels flourished on the
proceeds they received from the patronage of the
neighboring mining towns. The town was easily ac-
cessible from all Range points, and "parties" there
were likely to be safe from interference by authori-
ties, although there were four or five fully uni-
formed policemen on the main street every night. In
fact, one could walk a block or two and pass only
policemen. It is certain that they made no attempt
to curb illicit activities. Occasionally Federal
men visited the community, but these visits were usually communicated beforehand to the resort owners
by the usual "grapevine" method, with the result
that the Federal men succeeded in padlocking only
one or two places at a time. A visitor going
through main street in 1933 could observe four
places of business with padlock notices on their
doors which had been closed because of the violation of the Eighteenth Amendment.

If the resorts of Gilbert had depended on
local patronage, they would have been closed long
ago. The local residents know what goes on behind
the curtained windows of the "soft drink" parlors,
but they have built their homes in good faith and
naturally are reluctant to dispose of them when values have shrunk to almost one-fifth of the original
figures. Most of the sporting-house owners are of
Southern European stock. Today the patrons are the
younger men of the Range communities, out for a
"thrill," and traveling business men and other "respectable" men from distant points seeking secluded
revelry.

The situation in Gilbert represents a read-
justment that takes place where labor is gone, but

where taxable resources are still present, so it is
not exactly typical of the final period in the history of the mining town. It is, however, suggestive
of the fact that new adjustments are made when labor, one of the three basic groups, leaves. If ore
had been previously exhausted, a large part of the
public that now lives by tax incomes would have had
to either seek a new means of livelihood or migrate.
As conditions now exist, only the business men have
had to make new adjustments. The successful ar-
rangement was found in carrying on two forms of il-
legitimate business, bootlegging and prostitution,
both of which drew trade from a large hinterland.

How Long Will Ore Last?

In the exploitation of Mesabi ore the policy
has been to take the best first. Disregarding this
fact for the moment, it is significant that Eveleth
had in 1930 passed the midway point in ore supply,
Hibbing had approximately reached it, and Virginia
had exhausted only a small portion of the supply
within the city limit.[2] The figures for Virginia
are deceiving, however, as the most active mine of
recent years is just outside the city limits in the
territory of the village of Franklin. The building
of Virginia had been partially due to this mine,
from which a large portion of the best ore has been
removed.

It took thirty-eight years to reach this
stage of development. How long will it take to ex-
haust the supply in Eveleth, Hibbing, and Virginia,
excluding the possibility of developing ore bodies
that are not now merchantable? Basing estimates
upon an average of the annual productions of iron
ore for the five years, 1926 to 1931 inclusive, we
find that if ore is produced in Hibbing for the next

2. See **Minnesota Mining Directory,** 1931.

seventeen years and four months at the same annual
rate at which it was produced for the above period,
the known supply of merchantable ore of 1930 will be
exhausted.[3] On the same basis, ore in Eveleth will
be exhausted in approximately twenty-two years and
in Virginia in one hundred fifty-five years. According to the average annual rate of shipment that has
persisted for the five years, (1926-1931) the present
known bodies of merchantable ore of the Mesabi will
be exhausted in thirty-two years.

The prediction for Virginia is high. This is
due to the fact that mines did not operate in Virginia during the five years used as the base period,
with the exception of the Minnewas Mine, which began
operations in 1930 and shipped over a million and a
half tons during the season.[4] At the 1930 rate of
production, Virginia ore supply will be exhausted in
fifty years.

There have been years when the Mesabi has
produced less ore, and years when it has produced
more ore, but the average annual production for the
fifteen-year period, 1916-1930, has been 35,031,332
tons. At this rate, the supply of ore will last only
thirty-three years. The average annual production
for the thirty-year period, 1901-1930, has been
28,612,456 tons, which means that if this same rate
persists, the ore will last only forty years. Even
if we take the average rate of production since the
first ton of ore was shipped from the Mesabi and assume that future productions will average no more,
Mesabi ore will last only fifty-two years.

The most conservative prediction, based on
the past developments, indicates that by 1980 the

---

3. Ibid.
4. The Mesabi Mountain Mine in the village of Franklin, bor-
   ders the city limits of Virginia, and has been the largest
   ore producer in the world. It has produced an average of
   approximately five million tons annually, 1926-1930, and
   has a remaining tonnage of over twenty-three million.

Mesabi will be stripped of all its present known supply of merchantable ore.   In fact, an estimate based
on production of the last fifteen years, which probably indicates more nearly future conditions, suggests that the good ore will be exhausted by 1963.

The quality of iron ore on the Mesabi Range
has decreased from 56.07 per cent iron in 1902 to
51.19 per cent in 1929. For the last ten years,
however, the quality has remained about constant,
due largely to the use of various "beneficiation"
devices.

Estimates place Minnesota's possible low-
grade ore reserves at 40,300,000,000 tons, or approximately one-half of the known world supply of
ores that are at present considered non-merchantable
in their Natural state.[5] The low-grade ores that
will be used first are those that can be mined by
the cheap open pit method. Most of these ores are
on the Mesabi Range. It is estimated that there are
9,447,500,000 tons of low-grade ores on the Mesabi
that can be mined by open pit methods and "beneficiated."[6] These ores average about thirty-five
per cent iron and are found to a depth of 400 feet,
but most of them cannot be "beneficiated" by known
methods. However, inventions may not be far distant
which will make this possible. There is also the
ever-present threat that tax rates will make "bene-
fication" unprofitable, and that new and more distant fields can be exploited with greater profit.

Wherever one places his estimate, regardless
of the degree of success in developing low-grade
ores, it is obvious that the days of the Mesabi
towns are numbered. The greatest iron range of all
history will some day, perhaps during the next generation, be worthless and desolate. Its technological culture will doubtless fade away gradually.

---

5. Warner, F. S., _Future Movement of Iron Ore and Coal in Re-_
    lation to the St. Lawrence Waterway, 1930.
6. Lake, M. C., _Mining and Metallurgy_, Aug., 1926.

P A R T   III

CULTURAL CHANGE IN THE MESABI TOWNS

    A. Pioneer Folkways and Mores
    B. Culture Building during the
       Period of Extravagance

Chapter VII

A. Pioneer Folkways and Mores

THE REALISTIC NATURE OF PIONEER FOLKWAYS[1]

The first concern of men who are facing nature in the rough is to supply basic organic needs.
The primary necessities, food, shelter, and sex satisfaction are first provided. Extras, in the way of
material improvements, come later.

Food

Fortunately for the pioneers the North woods
was bounteous in game, fish, and wild berries. Both
lumber and mining camps always had deer and moose
meat, regardless of seasons or laws. Eveleth residents were said to have lived mostly on moose meat
during their first winter.[2] Fish were secured by all
known means--nets, dynamite, and by less wasteful
methods. Later, communication was established with
the outside world so that food from many areas
could be shipped in. The ability to purchase food
shifted attention to earning and spending wages.

Industry

The prospectors preceded the settlers and
located ore bodies. The extent of the deposits were

---

1. See Ch. 5 for a summary of historical data on which most
   of the generalizations of this chapter are based. Also
   Woodbridge, op. cit.; Van Brunt, op. cit.
2. Van Brunt, op. cit., ch. 2.

for the most part unknown. The method of test pitting was crude compared to later methods, but required an extensive output of human energy. A well
was sunk in the stony soil by means of pick and
shovel, and the refuse was windlassed out. The forests had to be shaved from the surface of the soil,
shafts sunk for bringing out the ore, and railroads
extended to lake shore points some sixty miles away
before ore could be marketed at the lower lake
ports a thousand miles distant. Individual enter-
prisers with large capital reserves backed these
projects so that labor was provided with work and
wages.

Merchandising

        The mining company store provided necessi-
ties in pioneer days. Newcomers to the Range needed
credit, as well as food, clothing, and tools, and
the companies could furnish it in return for labor.
The company store was in the nature of a monopoly,
and quite often charged exorbitant prices for foods
and mining supplies. Companies frequently required
the men to buy at their store even after private
merchandising had become the rule. The month's expense account was deducted from the pay check.[3]
        Because there were wages, merchandising be-
came profitable, and a merchant class appeared in
the mining towns. As early as 1898, merchants in
Hibbing protected themselves against the company
store, and against the companies which designated
certain private stores as the places for their men
to trade. An unsuccessful move was set on foot for
securing legislation to make the company store illegal. The company stores, however, rapidly disappeared after 1900.
        Range prices were reputed to be high. A
protest was registered in the Sentinel of October

---

3. This was one of the issues of the strike of 1907. See
   ch. 15.

12, in 1895 to the effect that citizens were paying
twenty cents for kerosene while most places in the
state were paying ten cents and fifty cents for po-
tatoes while Princeton, Minnesota, paid ten cents.
Editorial comment suggested that the difference
could not all be attributed to freight rates. A
commercial public had apparently arrived to exploit
labor.

Shelter

Shelter was a serious problem in northern
Minnesota where frosts are likely to occur monthly
and where winter temperatures frequently range far
below the zero point. Even in summer, nights are
cool and rainfall is heavy. Nature provided fuel in
abundance, thus solving this problem for the set-
tler.

The men who plotted the Range towns brought
with them fixtures for small sawmills; so construction began with the clearing of the town plats.
Some of the buildings were made of logs, but most
of them were made of unplaned lumber which the mills
provided from virgin pine forests. A common type of
dwelling was the boarding house where a large number of male residents lived.

The towns were characterized by board sidewalks, ungraded streets, and crudely constructed
outdoor privies. Even the business blocks were of
frame construction--poor guarantee against the forest fires that ravaged the woods during dry seasons,
or even against fires that might originate within
the towns.

Sex Satisfaction

In the nineties the Range population was
largely men who had left their families in the old

country or in their former homes in this country.
The primitive life attracted a large number of the
unmarried from abroad as well as from more settled
parts of America. These men came to the Range lured
by the opportunities a mining community offers: hard
work, attractive wages, and the hope of stumbling
onto a fortune.

The pioneer communities were, in their inception, communities without homes. Few women with
families ventured there. Those married men who had
families did not bring them until the basic needs
of life were provided. The frontier, however,
proved to be a favorite spot for women who commer-
cialized sex.

The prostitute substituted for home and family for married men of the pioneer mining communities. She furnished satisfaction for all male
groups.

Relaxation

In the same wagons that carried the prospec-
tive miners and lumbermen to the North country and
in the same crowds traveling on foot were the liquor
merchants with their wares of trade, the gamblers
carrying their games and devices, and the prostitutes. Almost every other building that was erected on the main streets of the towns housed a saloon
with its backroom gambling dens and upstairs quar-
ters for the prostitutes. There seems to be a cor-
relation between primitive mining communities where
hard manual labor is the means of lucrative employment and equally intense and vicious forms of amusement. The Range fits this picture.

It used to be the custom of the single men
in the boarding houses to hurry off to the saloons
Saturday evening and arrive home just in time to
change clothes and report for work at the mines Monday morning. The chief amusement center provided
was the saloon.

As the basic needs of life were met, men turned toward conveniences, developed civic pride and community consciousness. This desire gathered momentum as the non-mining public increased in the Range communities. Soon new material culture sprang up to break the hard realities of the frontier.

However, as long as the pioneer characteristics of the communities remained, the fundamental problems of their residents of a few years later were of no concern. City halls, public works, pavement and utilities, recreational facilities, parks, playgrounds, and ornamental culture, libraries and brick school buildings, tax rates and tax levies, were little thought of by the pioneers. In fact, the State did not consider an adequate tax on iron ore until 1907.

Chapter VIII

THE TOLERANT NATURE OF PIONEER MORES

Many men who were attracted to the Mesabi
frontier had probably never been dominated fully by
the mores of any community. This is indicated by
the frequent reports of escaped convicts, thieves,
men who had deserted families, and those who for
other reasons had sought the seclusion of the mining
camps. Notwithstanding, there were undoubtedly
others in the lot who had previously maintained
high personal standards and had demanded reputable
mores in the communities from which they had come.
But standards suffered in the mining camps, and many
forms of behavior were tolerated, if not directly
sanctioned, that would have been condemned and outlawed elsewhere. The coming of complete families in
considerable numbers alone changed the frontier
codes.
Let us consider briefly behavior traits
that reflect pioneer mores.

Respectability of Saloon Keeper and Saloon

The saloon owner of this day was considered
a respectable business man of the city and was a
very powerful figure in the administration of its
affairs. He controlled politics in the city of Virginia through the "lumber jack" vote in the early
days and was to be reckoned with in every election.
Early settlers tell of the streets being crowded with
drunken "lumber jacks" in the spring of every year,
who had received their winter's earnings and boarded

the first train to the town to get to the saloons
as soon as possible. The women were there to receive them and encourage them in drinking at the bar.
The "jack" would wake up three or four days later
with a splitting headache and empty pocketbook, having been "rolled" by the bartenders or female hang-
ers-on around the saloons. Then the penniless "jack"
would be kicked out of the saloons because he no
longer possessed resources for exploitation by their
agents. The streets and saloon fronts would be
lined with penniless "jacks," with nowhere to go except to the city jail, there to be lodged and fed
at city expense. On election day they were treated
to drinks and told how to vote.

   One reason for the respectability of the
saloon is that there was no other community center
to which homeless men could go when the day's work
was done and on holidays and Sundays. Consequently
men gathered there not only to drink but to spend
their social evenings. While hard drinks were sold,
many a man patronized the bar only to buy soft
drinks. To be seen swinging the portals of the
saloon was not considered below the dignity of the
respectable citizen. The drink itself doubtless had
its attraction for the majority of the patrons. The
Sentinel reported in 1895 that over a carload of
"Fitcher's Beer" was consumed daily in Hibbing. There
were thirty saloons in the village at that time, and
they were reported to be increasing at the rate of
one a day.

   It is interesting to note that with the coming of the moving picture theater, saloons declined
considerably in popularity in the Range towns.

Accepted Behavior

   A news item from the Sentinel of February
22, 1894, indicates that drunkenness was accepted
as the commonplace.

There is a false idea afloat in foreign towns
that the residents of mining districts are no respec-
tors of law and order and are generally tough. We are
prepared to nail that false belief by an illustration
from Hibbing. Thursday, February 15, was pay day at
several of the mines and also at the mill. It is needless to say that the boys all "took in the town" and
enjoyed themselves to the full limit, and yet not a
single arrest was made, nor a complaint registered. The
boys were out for a time and had it, and we can say,
from personal knowledge, that they were more gentleman-
ly drunk or sober than a party of swell "guys" of the
city would be under the same circumstances.

A similar comment from the press of March 15,
1894, indicates that the election of that time must
have been pretty well celebrated. It reads:

With 200 inebriated men election evening, it is
strange there were no accidents. Everyone seemed to
"feel their oats" but no arrests were made and nothing
occurred worthy of note.

The standard of morality was none too high.
According to the news story the entire village
flocked down to the station once a day to see the
train come in. "Passengers, male and female, were
subjected to a gauntlet of remarks, some of them not
free from profanity and innuendo, as they alighted
from the train."[1]
Prostitutes in those days, according to informants, did not seclude themselves from public
view in daylight on the streets. There was no shame
in their vocation, for a considerable part of the
female population could be labeled demimonde.
Prostitutes were not respected by all but
were, apparently, tolerated. An editorial in the

1. Miles, Carlton, "The Romance of the Ranges," Minneapolis
   Journal, May 2, 1926.

Hibbing Sentinel of 1894 (June 2) suggests that the
editor was not fully in accord with the toleration
policy. He comments:

> The charge against Mrs. Hannan of keeping a house
> of prostitution was dismissed in Justice Robinson's
> court Tuesday--and mighty rank "justice" everybody
> thought it to be.

Tolerance of Illegal Enterprises

Games of chance were always in violation of
the law, so gambling dens were, from the beginning,
subject to raids by county officials. Many an ex-
pensive roulette wheel, slot machine, or other gambling device was seized in the towns.

The Grand Jury, meeting in Duluth in 1899,
reported:

> We find that the president and council of the vil-
> lage of Hibbing have allowed and suffered gambling to be
> carried on openly in several saloons and hotels of the
> said village; that gambling devices of the most common
> and notorious kind have been allowed to be openly exhib-
> ited in said saloons and hotels and that they have been
> used for the purpose of gambling and that they have been
> maintained for the purpose of getting the laboring men
> of the village and locality to waste and squander their
> earnings; that the village has been infested with pro-
> fessional gamblers and confidence men from the whole
> Northwest and in the opinion of this jury the village
> has become the rendezvous of the crime and corruption
> of St. Louis County; that this state of affairs has
> been made possible by reason of the consent, sufferance,
> if not the assistance of, T. Walde Murphy, the presi-
> dent of the village, and A. A. French, policeman and
> night watchman.[2]

---

2. Hibbing Sentinel, November 11.

Later, $ 2000 worth of gambling paraphernalia
was taken in a sheriff's raid on five places, and
fines totaling $604.65 were inflicted.

In addition, there were the illegal boxing
matches, forbidden by state laws, and enforced by
county officials. Nevertheless, the mining towns
had their boxing matches frequently.

Even the sale of liquor in Hibbing was for a
time forbidden by law due to an early Federal treaty
with the Indians, but it was only when Federal en-
forcement officers were on the scene that saloons
were closed.

Low Evaluation of Life

Protection of life reaches its highest development where there is feeling of responsibility
for others. A male community treats life careless-
ly and blots it out more freely. The Range communities had suicides altogether out of proportion in
the early days, many unnecessary industrial accidents, and deaths from intoxication and exposure.
The following glimpses from news items suggest the
nature of the situation.

Brown had dinner at Daigle's hotel, after which he
declined to go out to camp and complained that he was
sick. He was supplied with a bed and Doctor Butchart was
summoned and prescribed for him. On Monday the man died
and was removed to Barrett's Morgue by order of Deputy
Coroner Walker, who examined the body and decided that
an inquest was unnecessary. The deceased was about forty
years old and nothing is known of his friends or relatives. There was nothing of value on his person and the
only inkling as to his name was the employment agent's
card which was made out to Geo. Brown. The body will be
buried today.[3]

---

3. The Sentinel, 1899.

A man about forty-five years of age fell down a shaft and was instantly killed.

The deceased had worked at the Pillsbury only a month or so, and there is no information as to the whereabouts of his relatives.[4]

An old logger is quoted as saying:

But the old days when we came down from the woods were glorious ones. For the first week we always owned the town. The constable and sheriff either had business about that time in some neighboring town or locked themselves up in their houses. The wild dissipation we indulged in and the amount of villainous whiskey we consumed would kill anyone except one possessed with a constitution such as a winter's campaign in the woods insures. The boisterous laughter and the maddening yell must have been anything but reassuring to the peaceful citizens. To their credit be it said, however, those rough loggers were as a rule a good-natured gang, and did not molest anyone unless some overzealous officer attempted to interfere. Then there was trouble. The way a good part of the winter's wages was squandered in a few days was a shame....After a spree we often went back to work on the drives. Of all the work I ever did, log driving was the hardest....Submerged wholly or partly in ice-cold water with no chance to change clothes, there is little wonder that we all have rheumatism until we are certain our backs are broken and that our arms and legs will drop off. A busy summer at the mill, a visit to the harvest fields and in the fall we were back again in the woods. Lucky if we had a good knit suit and sufficient clothes.[5]

---

4. Ibid.
5. Ibid., Jan. 29.

Protection

Industry was careless with men in the early
days on the Range.[6] Primitive justice in settling
personal quarrels was frequently resorted to. There
were few provisions for caring for health and few
regulations to protect a man against the vices into
which he had fallen. Life from the protective
standpoint was very much on an individualistic basis
on the frontier; therefore, casualties were numerous.

Religion

The mining frontier had little interest in
religion; work was the dominant interest. It is
true, however, that missionaries soon came to the
mining camps and attempted to give them the sanctity
of religious worship. Little data exists regarding
the nature of religious work on the Mesabi in the
nineties, but suffice it to say that the press of
the time gave it little prominence.

Democracy

All men had status in these frontier communities. There was no noticeable discrimination because of caste or class. Race and nationality, religious creed, moral code, and fraternal attachments
were awarded no prizes and brought no disgrace. Any
one who could work was an accepted member of the
community, for numbers meant more than quality.

A Finnish lady, a long-time resident of the
Range, in an interview gave the following analysis of
the change in nationality sentiment:

---

6. The accident rate was excessive on the Mesabi until around
   1910.

Regarding racial prejudices, there was little difference in races or nationalities in the pioneer days. All
were interested in making a living and in building up the
community. Hard work was the order of the day, and a man
was accepted for face value according to his contribution
to the community, not his religion or nationality. As
leisure time has been diffused among the laboring classes
the nationality prejudices have manifested themselves.
Today each nationality is highly conscious of its superi-
ority over the others. Each nationality has its societies, and every year sees these activities and societies
grow stronger and more popular.

Shaking Off Pioneer Mores

As life became more stable, the old mores
were gradually condemned and were slowly replaced by
new codes.[7] The morals of the mining towns had been
loose. The second decade saw prostitution and gambling banished, the Sunday and all-night saloon forbidden, the number of saloons limited to a given
unit of population, and pure food laws introduced.
Life took on new meaning to the residents--
the careless exploitation of labor, the careless
licentious living, and the low evaluation of life
gradually disappeared. The masses gradually became
aware of community independence from the mining industry. They came to demand a share in ore aside
from wages--the benefits that come through protection, taxation, and public services. In this manner
they prepared the way for the lavish culture built
during the conflict period.

---

7. See the latter part of ch. 4.

Chapter IX

B. Culture Building during the Period of Extravagance

COMMUNITY GRATIFICATION THROUGH PUBLIC SERVICES

In contrast to the primitive folkways of the pioneer period, the conflict period in the Range towns saw the growth of extensive public works and the building of lavish public institutions. These developments are significant indices of the folkways of the period. In this chapter a brief survey of the material culture of Range towns is made with a view to indicating the extent to which public services were developed for the citizens of the municipalities. The most important municipal services are: public utilities, educational facilities including schools and libraries, and recreational facilities. These are discussed in the order named.

Public Utilities

Since around 1912 no one of the three Range towns has lacked anything in the way of ordinary public utilities. In addition to cement sidewalks, which replaced the board walks of pioneer times, the streets were paved and after that was accomplished the alleys were paved. Not only were streets lighted with electricity, but elaborate white ways with five lights to the lamp post were laid out to decorate the cities. At the close of the Seabold presidency Hibbing boasted of more white ways than could Cleveland, Ohio, a city over twenty-five times as large. Not only were mechanical fire trucks purchased, but

fire halls were built, and enough firemen were employed to have three shifts, each group working eight
hours. (Most other cities at that time were working
two shifts daily, each group working ten hours.)
Hibbing and Virginia each built municipal gas plants
where artificial gas was produced. Beautiful city
halls were erected. Greenhouses were built to provide flowers and shrubs for the parks. Zoological
parks were established in each municipality and
stocked with animals. Public rest rooms were provided for the farmers. Municipal nurseries were established for the children of working mothers.
Hibbing went so far as to build potato warehouses,
where the farmers temporarily disposed of their po-
tatoes. The village in turn took the responsibility
of sending them to the local merchants. Besides
these warehouses the city maintained a municipal
barn and a market place.[1] On July 4-5, 1931, Hibbing dedicated a 160-acre municipal airport. Virginia also has an airport, valued at $87,000.

Perhaps the outstanding achievement in
public works has been the development of municipal
heating plants in each of the towns. In Hibbing and
Eveleth heat has been largely confined to the business sections; Virginia has extended heat to residences in all parts of the city except the section
north of the railway tracks.[2]

It is also Virginia that has achieved national recognition for the successful operation of munic-
ipally-owned public utilities. It had the lowest
electric rates in America in 1931.

Education

Educational institutions have grown both in
numbers and in architectural grandeur in each of the

---

1. See also historical editions of newspapers in each of the
   towns.
2. See Minnesota Municipalities. 1931,pp.226-229; 280-285;
   292-294, for number of customers and rates charged for
   various utilities in the three towns.

Range towns. During pioneer times school buildings
were small frame structures that soon became over-
crowded because of the high birth rate among immigrant families. As the years passed and the large
numbers entering the primary grades gradually rose
from grade to grade, buildings had to be erected almost annually. It was estimated that in 1932 the
peak load for the high school would end and that
thereafter the number of high school pupils would
decline.

The population factor is back of the material development of the school system. There are
other factors such as the growth of community pride
in public buildings, financial prosperity, extravagance mores, inter-range-town rivalry, etc., that
help to explain the type of school buildings that
were developed.

The population aspect of the school program
suggests that in the near future there are likely to
be vacant school buildings, fewer teachers and a
complete cessation of the building program, thus re-
versing the growth trend that characterized the
school systems of the three Range towns until 1930.

The school building program was at one time
hindered somewhat by mining company protests. However, the tonnage tax agitation in 1909 did considerable to get the mining company's support for
better schools. The Range people joined hands with
them to fight the tonnage tax, the proceeds of which
were to go to the State treasury. The argument used
was that such excessive State taxation would rob the
Range schools of their necessary support. At this
time the mining companies sanctioned the building of
a high school; also of two frame structures for
primary schools.

The Hibbing Junior college came in 1921-1922
and grew rapidly from an initial enrollment of forty
in 1921 to an enrollment of 350 in 1931. Teacherages
have been built in the outlying locations of the
district. Busses have been employed to bring

students to the centralized schools. Texts, paper,
pencils, and musical instruments are provided by
the schools. No tuition is charged, even in the
junior college.

The Hibbing School District (Number 27) covers six full townships and eight sections of a seventh township. It is twenty-four miles long and
twenty miles wide. The assessed valuation is
$28,000,000, about 95 per cent of which is derived
from the iron mines located in the immediate vicinity of Hibbing. Hibbing claims to have the largest
and most costly high-school building in the world.
This building has a frontage of 416 feet and has
three wings, the longest of which is 265 feet.
It has two gymnasiums, a swimming pool, large study
hall, library, splendid auditorium, botanical con-
servatory, large cafeteria, the general offices of
the school districts, a suite of rooms for the
school dentist, doctor and nurses, and open-air
rooms for pupils of frail health. There is a ten-
acre site for athletic grounds in the vicinity.

The curriculum includes the following:
foundry, forging, machine shop, automobile and gas
engine, agriculture, assaying, mineralogy, survey-
ing, printing, normal school training, biology,
physics, chemistry, botany, bookkeeping, typewrit-
ing, shorthand, art, music, sewing, cooking, mil-
linery, dressmaking, mathematics, history, engineer-
ing, geography, Latin, French, Spanish, economics,
and civics.

A phase of education not found in the ordinary community, but one which is highly developed
in the Range towns, is adult education and citizen-
ship training. Probably in no other section of
Minnesota has adult education been carried to such
perfection as in these towns. This is due to the
large number of Europeans who have been drawn to
the mines. Those responsible for education soon
realized the necessity of Americanizing these foreigners. Every school district can boast of an en-
viable record in their Americanization programs. No

expense on the part of the schools was spared; every
possible facility was utilized. Civics, American
government, United States history, and English were
the principal subjects taught.

Second to the school system only are libraries in the scheme of Range education. Each of
the towns has libraries housed in well-built brick
buildings, that provide books in many languages, a
special children's reading room, and special parlors
for club meetings and social gatherings. In each
town the library developed after the passing of the
pioneer period, and reached its peak during the
period of extravagance in culture building.

The traveling library plan, which has attracted nation-wide interest to the Hibbing library,
is unique. The traveling library bus or "Book Wagon"
is six and one-half feet wide, fifteen feet long and
six feet high. It is built to carry twelve hundred
books and seats ten people, including·driver and librarian. Benches are placed in it back to back for
the use of customers, drivers and librarian. In its
travels the bus covers an area of 160 miles reaching
twenty-five locations. Most of the locations are
visited once a week; a few of the smaller ones are
visited every other week.

Municipal Recreation Facilities

Beginning about 1912 the Range cities took
on an extensive recreation program sponsoring winter
sports, hockey, curling, and winter sport festivals.

Each town, previous to the per capita limitation law, financed baseball, and hockey teams.
Eveleth built a combined auditorium, armory, and community recreation building in 1912 at a cost of
$25,000. In 1918 a recreation building for skating
and curling was erected at a cost of $125,000. In
addition a hippodrome of wooden construction built
on huge dimensions was erected. The other two towns

followed with combination recreation and auditorium
buildings in memory of the World War dead.

Dances seem to be the order of the day insofar as recreation is concerned. The recreation
building in Virginia has four or five dances every
week--ten cents admission and four hours of dancing.
Eveleth has the same. Hibbing has very little dancing in the summer, but frequently has ten-cent
municipal dances in the winter.

The dance floors of the recreation buildings
in the three towns are converted into ice-skating
rinks during the winter months, although they have
hardwood floors; they are covered with roofing paper
and sand and then flooded. The Hibbing arena has a
composition floor which is flooded during the winter
months. Adjoining the rinks are heated rest rooms.
In addition to the arena there are outside skating
rinks in practically all the school yards throughout
the cities.

Due to the large financial resources of the
Range school districts, all schools have built the
most modern and fully equipped gymnasiums, swimming
pools, athletic fields, and auditoriums. Great
stress is placed upon school athletics. No expense
is spared to get the best coaches and instructors.
Swimming instruction is given the year around in the
two pools in the Virginia schools.

Then, each town has well-developed parks.
The Eveleth Memorial Park, containing six acres, was
laid out in 1913. Here the library is located and
here weekly band concerts are held in summer. Another park, located on the north side, is primarily
a children's summer playground. The tourist park is
located on Eveleth Park Lake, overlooking St. Mary's
and Eveleth Lakes. Here swimming facilities and
equipment for camping are provided. The facilities
of the tourist camp are available to all at a daily
charge of fifty cents. In 1911 the Oliver Iron
Mining Company donated fifty-five acres to the city
of Virginia to be used as a park. This area became

Olcott Park, and the city immediately planted it
with trees and shrubbery. Some 10,000 trees were
planted, thirty-five miles of boulevard laid out,
flower gardens prepared, and a zoo arranged, turning
the area into a playground and recreation center. The
South Side Park was opened a few years later. Municipal band concerts are held twice a week during the
summer months in these two parks.

As early as 1905 Virginia had established a
public park system. In the reorganization of the
government in 1909 a Park Commission was created to
have charge of the park system.

Early in 1915 visitors pronounced Hibbing
park system the best in the state, considering the
expenditures involved. Conrad Wolf, an expert land-
scape gardener who was park superintendent under
the Seabold administration, is given much of the
credit for its development. The Mesabi Park was located in the heart of the village and the Bennet
park, south of the village. Since Hibbing was
moved, Bennet park stands between North and South
Hibbing. Here is a public greenhouse, a zoo, flower
gardens, shrubbery and trees. It is an ideal recreation center in good weather, wood and fireplaces
being provided for picnics.

The greatest private venture in Hibbing recreation was the Oliver Club, established by the
Oliver Iron Mining Company in 1908 and opened December 25. This provided a recreation center for
Oliver employees of the district. A similar club was
established in Virginia about the same time.

The Hibbing recreation budget voted for 1926
amounted to $34,479.91. A salary of $3500 was paid
a sports director, and $2500 each was paid a man
and woman assistant.

Summarizing, the culture of the period of
extravagance presents a contrast to that of the
pioneer period. Public utilities, which were of little concern to the pioneers, were extensively developed during this time.

Chapter X

PERVERSIONS IN SPENDING

Communities whose social classes do not con-
tribute equal shares to tax moneys find it difficult
to get the most in returns from public expenditures.
This is especially true when conflict is the dominant attitude existing between the spending group
and the tax-paying group. We wish now to consider
perversions in spending that seem to grow out of
the conflict relations between the industrial taxpayer and the spending community.

It was in the year 1912 when Victor Seabold
came to the presidency of Hibbing as the choice of
the people that extravagance began. Previous to
this time the office was held by Dr. Ray, a conservative man, who was associated with the hospital which
received the workingman's monthly health fees
through the Oliver Mining Company. The attitude had
prevailed in the village that the Oliver Company
was the best friend the community had, and that the
people should strive to maintain friendly relations
with it. Citizens had put up with inconveniences
and dangers to maintain the harmonious relationship,
but Seabold, in taking an antagonistic attitude,
brought the conflict to the surface.

In three years Seabold had multiplied expenditures more than four times. Hibbing had become
more than a million-dollar village. An official of
one of the mining companies commenting upon Seabold's
administration in an interview with the writer said,
"They could have paved the streets out of silver
dollars here for all the money they have grafted."

Note the change in expenditures under the
old and new regimes.[1]

COMPARATIVE EXPENDITURES

Year	Expenditures	Receipts
1910	$ 303,152.13	$ 333,850.02
1911	282,292.25	340,751.86
1912	484,960.10	327,979.09
1913	773,062.10	417,125.07
1914	1,233,728.54	902,789.76

A mining-company politician called attention[2] to the fact that for a ten-year period Hibbing,
a village of 15,000 population, spent more than
Duluth, a city of 100,000 population. He said further, "Many illegal expenditures are permitted in
the Range towns that would never be permitted in any
other towns."

A large indebtedness began in Hibbing with
Seapold's presidency. Continued additions brought
the total to approximately four million at the close
of his ten-year term. Obligations totaling
$3,428,344.00 remained in January, 1931.[3]

Eveleth also had a period of extravagant
spending which led to the accumulation of burdensome
debts. Obligations totaling $463,959.00,[4] were re-
vealed by an audit in January, 1931. The public
examiner, on reviewing the books in 1929,[5] found
that the city was about one year behind in paying
current bills. It was making no provision for the
payment of outstanding debts, although the expenditures in 1930 could not exceed $70 per capita. The
city had also suffered a loss of $4,000,000 in valu-
ation in the preceding ten years.

---

1. Schedule 2, Report of Public Examiner, 1916.
2. In an interview with the writer.
3. Minnesota Yearbook, 1921, pp.212-218.
4. Ibid.
5. Ms. of 163 pp., on file in Office of State Public Examiner,
   St. Paul.

The mining companies, in a report to the State
Tax Commission in 1928, presented the following statistics on obligations of mining towns in Minnesota.[6]

PER CAPITA MUNICIPAL INDEBTEDNESS

Municipal Indebtedness:	1925	1926	1927
Mining district	234.51	220.89	200.41
Balance of Minnesota	65.33	-	-
Entire United States	75.06	-	-

It is apparent that municipal expenditures
have been lavish, even to the extent of exceeding
the abundant tax revenues.

The extensive development of the material
side of education came about after 1910. This development coincides with the appearance of the dominant
conflict pattern. To secure greater benefits from
ore, for the public and for labor, lavish expenditures carried developments far beyond the point of
necessity. The common question with school boards
came to be, "How much can we spend?", not "Where can
we save?" As one Range superintendent expressed it,
"In other communities where I have worked the basic
question at all board meetings was 'Where can we cut
expenses?'. here the first question is, 'Is that all
we can levy?'"[7]

As a result, the fame of Range education has
spread far and wide. People who know nothing more
of the Mesabi towns have heard of their schools. The
traveler in even the smallest range municipality is
amazed to see its beautiful and costly school buildings. Virginia claims to have one of the finest
technical high schools in existence; Eveleth has a
similar one, and Hibbing has achieved school fame by

6. Exhibit "C" of Mining Companies Report to State Tax Commission; See 1930 Report State Tax Commission.
7. Statement made to the writer in an interview, 1932.

owning what is alleged to be one of the finest high-
school structures in the world.

Expenditures have not stopped at the legitimate and legal. Public works for which there was
no legal authority in municipal charters have been
constructed and managed.[8]

There is considerable evidence that Hibbing
and Eveleth politicians have tried to extend public
services gratis to many. Eveleth had eight paid
engagements for the auditorium and 350 gratis engagements for 1916, while the recreation building
records showed one paid engagement and 110 gratis
engagements.[9]

The Eveleth water department, in 1929, had
fifty-one customers on its free list, had large sums
in uncollected bills, and was operating at an annual
net loss of $32,583.33.[10] The same situation ob-
tained in Hibbing for many years.[11] In many cases a
discount of 50 per cent was allowed on bills.

Range towns have acted like individuals who
suddenly fall heir to immense wealth, and spend lav-
ishly, even seeking new fields of expenditure to
dispose of their money. Each town is the center of
immense ore reserves, which in themselves create a
taxable asset of immense value; the mines have been
levied upon freely. The local residents seldom objected to tax rates because the taxes they paid in-
dividually were increased tenfold by mining tax revenues.

Thus, residents of the Range find the lavish
spending of tax moneys for the public weal perfectly
natural. The individual who has wealth seldom lives
as though he were a pauper. Why should the town with

---

8. The cutting remarks of the State Public Examiner, in his
   report on the affairs in Hibbing, prepared in 1922, is suggestive of conditions. The report is on file in the St.
   Paul office of the State Public Examiner.
9. See typed reports of the State Public Examiner on file in
   the St. Paul office.
10. Ibid.   11. Ibid.

wealth live as though it possessed little? Then
there is ever present the thought expressed by an
Eveleth fireman: "Why shouldn't these towns have
everything they want? If we don't get it, it will
go to New York to buy cigars for the damn capitalists down there. All we'll have left anyway is big
holes in the ground out there." When one considers
the wealth of the towns, he is surprised that they
do not spend far more. Perhaps the most amazing
thing of all is that with all their taxable assets
the towns are frequently burdened with debt and at
times are seriously embarrassed by a shortage of
city funds.

Hibbing closed its first year by ordering
bills totaling $1,653.99 paid. Twenty-five years
later bills were totaling well over a million dollars annually. The Auditor's Report of 1929 showed
a levy of $1,994,337.32 for Hibbing, yet in the
year 1929, Hibbing was very embarrassed financially.
The long period of conflict drove the town to
spending extremes that have been incorporated in
the mores of the community and in the habits and
tastes of the citizenry. These practices have
gathered momentum with the years, and legal restrictions have not been sufficient to change long-established habits and customs.

Eveleth is, likewise, plunging forward into
annual litigation and injunctions; tax moneys are
exhausted a year ahead of time; large obligations
must be met by warrants. The citizens suffer for
want of intelligent and conservative leadership. The
mining companies have established restrictions by
the per capita law, but the community is still dominated by an urge toward extravagance.

Virginia has, on the other hand, fostered a
conservative policy, as mining towns go, and has
not been embarrassed by legislative measures or by
the depression. Her traditions of conservative management have, likewise, been cumulative and have
taken on the characteristic of a cultural compulsive.

What are the differential factors in the
situation?

Differential Spending

That the spending pattern in Virginia is
different from that in the other Range towns is at-
tested by varied types of evidence. First, the
comparative levies of the three towns for municipal
purposes may be cited. Hibbing, a village of approximately 15,000 population, has levied more than two
and a quarter millions of dollars in a single year.
For the last twelve years her annual levies have
averaged over two millions. Eveleth, with approximately 7000 population, levied well over a million
dollars in 1920. In the twelve years since it has
levied an aggregate of more than nine and a quarter
millions. Virginia has a much better tax record,
with an expenditure for the twelve years (1921-1932)
of about seven and one quarter millions. Virginia's population has averaged approximately 13,000
for the period.
Second, a comparison of financial obligations of the three towns shows that Virginia is the
most secure as far as debts are concerned. Her
small bonded indebtedness is not in undesirable li-
abilities but is simply an extension of credit to
people who have installed city heat. Hibbing and
Eveleth have heavy debts, totaling almost three and
one-half millions and almost a half million respectively.
A visitor to the three Range towns has difficulty in seeing a difference in services acquired
through the differential expenditures. Virginia has
about everything in the way of municipal and school
properties that a town could wish for. They are
not quite as lavish as are some Hibbing properties
but are far more attractive than Eveleth properties.
For years Virginia has spent much less money. The

difference is explained, in part, by the fact that
there is more efficient management.

Third, testimonial evidence given by Virginia
residents and by those of Hibbing and Eveleth is
abundant to the effect that Virginia is different in
its spending pattern.

The following explanation seems reasonable,
if not fully adequate:

Virginia is not a typical mining town. Up
to 1931, she had lumber mills which provided work
for 1300 men and a substantial tax income. Moreover, taxable.iron resources within the limits of
the city are relatively much smaller than for either
Hibbing or Eveleth. Hibbing's total valuation has
exceeded $90,000,000, Eveleth's $18,000,000, whereas Virginia's valuation has at no time exceeded
$21,000,000.[12] Virginia has been approximately
equal in size with Hibbing and about twice as large
as Eveleth.

There is another significant difference.
Local residents in Virginia have paid approximately
30 per cent of their taxes, whereas in Eveleth about
92 per cent and in Hibbing about 95 per cent have
been paid by mining companies.[13]

These combined differences, each of which
helps explain the other, cover a multitude of differences in spending habits. Virginia residents
have had vested interests in keeping expenditures
within the bounds of reason. Approximately a third
of the money being spent was their money. They
have elected and reelected men whom they could
trust to preserve their conservative traditions.
There has also been the factor of conflict in local
politics, which may have been largely accidental
in its origin, but which has been perpetuated
through the years. Previous to 1912 it centered
in vice policies. Subsequent to that time for a

12. State Auditor's Report.
13. Typewritten statement furnished by an Oliver Iron Mining
    Company official.

long period it centered in the question of the ownership of public utilities.   There have been no
major policies of difference since 1920, but the
dissention continues. Conflict within has hindered
the unifying of public forces against the mining
company; this has been a blessing in disguise.
Then the continuous clerkship of Alford Ford has
probably been an important factor in keeping affairs going straight.[14] Ford has kept books while
other city clerks have manipulated records to gain
desired ends.[15]

        The Hibbing and Eveleth publics have been
united against the mining companies. Mayors and
councils have worked together to get the most possible from public office. All the citizens asked was
a beneficient paternalism. For every dollar the
citizens paid in taxes the absentee owner paid between $90.00 and $95.00.

---

14. The Public Examiner complimented Mr. Ford for his efficient
    records in the only public examination the city has had;
    op. cit.
15. See Public Examiners Reports for Hibbing and Eveleth, op.
    cit.

Chapter XI

THE EVOLUTION OF THE ORE TAXATION POLICY

The tax complex is always a vital one in any
community but is exceedingly important in an iron-
mining municipality. This is true both when it involves the assessments on personal real estate and
private property and when it involves assessments
on corporation property and mineral resources. Fundamentally, the Range towns have faced two problems:
the first, that of insuring a sufficient local income from mining properties; the second, that of
shielding the mining companies from excessive taxation by the State. In reality these problems have
been one and the same. The matter of shielding the
mining companies from state taxes has not grown out
of any benevolent disposition on the part of the
municipalities toward the mining companies, but out
of a feeling that if more of the tax goes to the
State the smaller will be the share of the local
community. The State, on the other hand, is faced
with the problem of preserving for the commonwealth
a share of its natural heritage in iron ore through
tax revenues. The mining companies are interested
in the reduction of taxes with a consequent increase in profits.

Participation of Range Towns in Taxation Developments

In pioneer times little thought was given to
taxation either by the local communities or by the
State. Later the tax issue became a vital one in
which three groups were interested, the mining

companies, the State, and the Range towns. These
groups have participated in a triangular conflict
which has led to the present policy of taxation. In
the history of the Mesabi, the towns have been al-
lied at times with the mining companies and at other
times with the State. During the period from 1906
to 1920 the State was constantly attempting to get
a larger share of the taxes in opposition to the
Range municipalities, which united with the mining
companies. Since 1920 the mining companies have
been attempting to limit local taxes through the influence of the State legislature, so the policy of
the towns has been one of self-defense against en-
croachments both by mining companies and the State.

In the spring of 1915 the Harrison Bill was
a live issue. It called for a per capita limitation
of expenditures in municipalities of over 5000
population to $25.00 per year.

At that time the mining companies circulated
a pamphlet accusing eight of the Range villages of
raising more taxes proportionately than did 140
other villages and cities of the State. It was shown
that in the 140 towns per capita expenditures for
municipal purposes averaged $5.35 annually; for
Duluth $11.01; for St. Paul $11.20; and for Minneapolis $12.52; whereas for Hibbing it was almost
$100.00 per capita, or $500.00 for each family of
five. Hibbing at this time had a population of approximately 12,000, and during the year 1914 spent
approximately $1,200,000 (excluding school expendi-
tures)--more than the entire general levy of Duluth,
a city seven times larger. In spite of this high
levy, Hibbing's indebtedness had increased from
$284,792 in January 31, 1913 to $1,252,597, in January 31,1915. For the previous ten years taxes in
Hibbing had increased about twenty-seven times as
fast as had the population. The mining companies
were paying 98 per cent of the taxes. The same general story applied to several other Range towns,
namely Chisholm, Buhl, Keowatin, and Mountain Iron.

The Range people had another story. They
appealed to the legislature to protect them against
the aggression of the "millionaire mine owners of
the East." In the Hibbing Tribune of April 17,
1915 the arguments published were:

> Don't Forget: That Hibbing is an island, surrounded
> by yawning open pits and underlaid by iron ore—you can
> stand in the center of the business district of Hibbing
> and almost throw a baseball into four of the biggest
> open iron ore pits in the world—and mining operations
> account for by far the greater portion of Hibbing's ex-
> penditures. There has never been a year when Mining
> Companies were in control of Hibbing that they did not
> spend more than $25.00 per capita. Don't Forget: That
> the Mining Companies have bought men and newspapers and
> village councils from the Range to testify that this
> bill is fair—every one of which men or newspapers or
> councils are either mining officials or deeply involved
> with the Mining Companies. Don't Forget: That the Min-
> ing Companies say, "The per capita limit will affect
> only villages and cities on the Ranges"—neglecting to
> tell you that other parts of the bill will affect the
> bonding and taxing powers of every village and city in
> the state.[1]

Seabold was given most of the credit for
having defeated the Harrison Bill. He was called
"the Napoleon of Hibbing." On his return at 10:56
p.m., on the twenty-second of April, he was met by
a band, and a crowd with torchlights and fireworks.
The celebration lasted until morning. He was given
a big banquet in Hibbing, and his friends at that
time suggested that he run for the governorship.
This fight also proved a great publicity stunt for
Hibbing. Announcements of her white way and lavish
municipal expenditures were publicized throughout
the nation.

1. April 17, 1915.

Range attitudes on the local tax question
are well expressed in the **Mesabi Ore** of Hibbing.

The "Ore" believes that every cent possible
should be collected from the mining companies while they
are with us, to the end that we may retain unto ourselves a share of the wealth that, once removed, will
never return....we do not believe in waste or extravagance in municipal management or anywhere else, but we
shall hold that Hibbing should collect every year the
one and one-half million dollars due it from the mining
companies.

We owe it to ourselves to collect every cent
available from the taxation of these mines and use it to
beautify our towns because it belongs to us. Hibbing
surely receives no thanks for handing over a million
dollars a year of its own money to Eastern mine owners,
and we will be just as well treated if we collect and
spend all that is due us.[2]

Range citizens again sent hundreds of wires
to the governor protesting the per capita tax limitation law in 1921, which called for the reduction
of municipal expenditures to $50.00 per person. They
succeeded in raising the requirements to $100.00.
Despite their later attempts to have the law re-
pealed, it continued in force and was revised in
1929 calling for the following scale: 1929, $100.00
per capita; 1930, 1931, $80.00; 1932, $75.00; 1933,
and thereafter $70.00. Since 1929 the towns have
been concerned with the problem of keeping expenditures within the law.

Increasing Municipal Valuations by the
Annexation of Ore Properties

A device for increasing tax assessments frequently resorted to in Range towns has been that of

2. For a discussion of the various tax measures see the following reports of the Minnesota Tax Commission, 1928, chs.
   VIII-X, ch. 5.

annexing mining properties, so that they could be
covered by city tax assessments.

A few instances will illustrate that this
has not been an infrequent procedure. In 1905 districts northwest and south of Virginia voted themselves into the corporate limits of the city. This
move, led by the Virginia citizens doubled the assessed valuation of their town.

A news item in the Virginia Enterprise of
January 29, 1909, states the attitude of the Range
citizens toward annexation:

> The taking in by annexation all the property
> that was voted into the city limits in November, 1905,
> was the greatest "stunt" ever pulled off in this city,
> although but few taxpayers realized what a fight there
> was by a handful of citizens to accomplish it. It
> meant an increase in the real-estate valuation of the
> city of eight and one-half millions of dollars--that's
> all.

Even though Hibbing has annexed several
properties, her annexation problem has no doubt
been a less vital one than that of the other Range
towns. Hibbing has remained a village, even though
exceeding 15,000 population. This means that she
has spent a large part of the taxes of the Township
of Stunts. She has virtually all the surrounding
mining locations within her reach for a limited
amount of taxation.

The Evolution of State Taxation Policy

There is little question but that the Minnesota policy of ore taxation in the early days was
far too lenient for the good of the state. Taxes
have been increased through the years until many
groups feel that they are now too heavy for the good
of the mining industry. The combined taxes upon the
ore-mining industry have provided an annual state
revenue running beyond the twenty million mark.

Every tax measure favoring the State has
been gained in the face of paid lobbyists, working
for the mining industry, and opposition from the
Range towns. These measures have been maintained
only by rejecting company appeals for lowered taxation. An extensive appeal was made to the State Tax
Commission and appears in their 1928 report. It was
signed by sixteen mining companies and presented evidence to show that the best interests of the State
were to be attained through lowered taxes, thus preserving the mining industry and aiding its development of low-grade ores. We are not interested in
evaluating the state taxation policy, but simply in
pointing out the role of conflict in the evolution
of the system now in existence.

An Analysis of the Factors in the Evolution of the Ore Taxation Policy

Ore taxes at the present time are distributed in Minnesota as follows:[3]

Taxes	Per Cent State	Per Cent County and Municipality	Per Cent Trust Fund
Ad Valorem	10.5	69.5	–
Occupation	50	–	50
Royalty	100	–	–

Previous to 1921, the great bulk of the taxes
went to the local communities. Even at the present
time approximately three-fourths of iron ore taxes go
to county and local governments, since ad valorem
revenues are by far the largest.

Previous to 1912, the State was getting less
than a million dollars in ore taxes by which the local communities on the Range were almost entirely
supported. However, the mining communities had been

3. Purdee, J. S., The Children's Heritage.

able to maintain favorable south state opinion, and
there was little desire on the part of legislatures
to interfere with the welfare of the infant villages
or with the new industry. The messages to the legislators and governors from the Range communities and
from the mining companies were effective. Moreover,
the State had not learned to depend upon mineral income. The mining companies and local communities
worked together harmoniously, and the State was not
considered an enemy to either, except at times when
moves were made by certain groups in the legislature
to increase ore taxes.

After the conflict developed between the
Range towns and the mining companies, news of public
extravagance began to filter into sections of the
State beyond the Range. The Range towns publicized
their prosperity; they sought notoriety and fame
through public display. Moreover, the mining companies called attention of legislators to the extravagance of the towns; gossip circulated widely about
million dollar schools with gold doorknobs, and of
libraries with Persian rugs on the floors. Many similar stories, composed of fact and fiction, were
noised abroad.

The Range towns' use of tax money could not
but bring an unfavorable reaction. Legislatures,
composed largely of non-range residents, would not
stand by and see funds, to which they felt the commonwealth had a right, squandered. A perishable
heritage was the right of the State. Consequently,
there followed the legislation already described,
increasing State taxes and reducing local tax power.
About 1922, Hibbing began to realize where the publicity that had been circulated was leading and
turned about face. Since then it has been a Hibbing policy to hinder publicity that might create
attitudes unfavorable to the Range.

The mining companies have made little net
gain in the triangular struggle with local communities and the State. They have bridled the local

communities quite successfully by the per capita law,
but additional State taxes that were added at the
same time local expenditures were limited have absorbed what was gained through the limitation of local taxation.   Their future attack will doubtless
be focused upon reduced state taxation.   The Range
towns themselves have little to hope for in the way
of increased taxation privileges.   They have over-
stepped both with the mining companies and with the
state legislatures.

Chapter XII

THE DEVELOPMENT OF THE POLITICAL MORES

Governments of the three Range towns are and
always have been normal in their form of organization. They are far from normal, however, in governmental mores. The expedient policy has been practiced widely. The mores have been characterized by
a willingness to overlook any violation of standard
codes that would bring public or private gain at
the expense of the mining interests.

The philosophy of patronage has permeated
the thinking of the masses, and people have come to
expect that their personal needs and desires will
be gratified through those in public office. The
widespread practice of a paternalistic policy by
politicians has created a group-wide sense of dependence upon public resources, even at the expense
of individual initiative and enterprise.

The mores of a community are objectified in
its accepted policies and practices. We will first
try to learn what the community mores are and then
attempt to explain their appearance and widespread
acceptance.

What Are the Political Mores?

Spending versus Economy: Until recent years
economy has not been a campaign issue in politics.
"The full dinner-pail," "Seabold, Prosperity, Prog-
ress," and such slogans have been the keynote.   In
Chapters IX and X the spending pattern has been
described.   Extravagant spending has had the full

sanction of the local communities.

Political Consciousness: "Everything is
politics on the Range," is an expression one frequently encounters, and one need not be on the Range
long to become convinced of its truth. "In Southern
Minnesota, it means nothing to be on the school
board or in city office. Here it means everything,"
said a Range social worker. A minister emphatically
declared: "Politics is the curse of the Range."
Immediately upon entering the boundaries of St.
Louis County, one observes large signs "Vote for X
for Commissioner," "Vote for Z for Commissioner,"
etc., along all highways. Later the observer learns
that these signs have been prepared and erected by
paving contractors who have vested interests in getting their candidate elected.
        Sooner or later any climber in economic or
social life must reckon with the grim realities of
politics. The basic interest seems to be personal
gain and the obtaining of jobs for friends. Even
men who have higher motives are credited with graft
and patronage by the public.

The Spoils System: In practically all
fields of government, offices and jobs are subject
to the hazards of political appointment, as every
change in major political offices means a change in
a large group of appointive officers and workmen.
The political mores have long sanctioned this policy,
and it is only recently that there is any tendency
to eliminate it, even in those departments where
frequent changes are hazardous to public safety,
namely, police and fire departments. The spoils
system extends not only to appointive offices, but
to common labor. Whether or not one's "side" is in
has made a lot of difference.
        A newly-elected council in Virginia in 1932
dismissed all street and public building employees
and appointed its own men in their stead. In Hibbing the hazards of political jobs were illustrated

by a recent change in the school board, which was
followed by a wholesale dismissal of employees.
The spoils system mores have changed, after
years of agitation, concerning protective officers.
Police and firemen of Eveleth and Hibbing have recently been put on a civil service basis.

Paternalism: Paternalism has for years been
incorporated in the political mores. It has taken
two main forms, subsidizing business and subsidizing
labor. The one, that of aiding business enterprises
by patronage of the city, is clearly indicated by
testimonial evidence and by extensive records in the
official reports of the State Public Examiner.
The second form of paternalism is that of
hiring labor from public funds to a degree altogether out of proportion to the villages' needs for
labor. The Public Examiner's report for Hibbing in
1916 indicated that during the year 1914, when 1178
votes were cast for mayor, there were as many as
1011 men on the monthly payroll. During 1915, when
there were 1710 votes, the number of men on the
payroll was as high as 1296. Paying salaries, when
no work was done, paying telephone charges for private phones from city funds, and other violations
are cited.
Public parasitism has been exhibited in numerous lawsuits directed against the city. It is
also present in the public relief system. The effects in blighting individual initiative have been
realized to a considerable degree. In the words of
an Eveleth schoolman, "Everyone born in this town
feels that the city owes him a living just because
he was born here."
Local newspaper accounts tell of large numbers of lawsuits aimed at collecting funds from the
public treasury. We are not here concerned with
the justice or injustice of the many claims which
have annually come to the attention of the officials.
It is a rather interesting reflection on a community's attitude, since claims of this nature are so

frequently presented with no comeback of adverse public opinion from the taxpayers. People with real or
alleged injuries have been greatly encouraged in
presenting claims by the fact that many of them were
paid willingly by the communities. The recent tax
limitations imposed by the legislature has curbed
the liberal policy of city officials during the last
few years, and many claims have been rejected.

The mining companies have also been defend-
ants in many suits. The village and private parties
have tried again and again to recover funds from the
mining interests.

The problem of providing for the poor in the
three Iron Range towns has been solved by work relief. Since doles were given by Carnegie in the
nineties, comparatively little direct relief was
given until the depression of the thirties. The
method of relief has been that of city employment.
The tax incomes have usually made it possible to expand the payroll to almost any proportions, because
legitimate expenditures have been the extent of the
administration's use of money. When needless extravagance and waste have crept in, tax incomes have
been devoured, and crises have found the cities
faced with the necessity of cutting the payroll. A depression instance is to the point. Eveleth had to
cut her city payroll mercilessly in 1933 and had to
depend upon the schools to carry the heavy load of
employment. With wise expenditures during the depression years citizens of Eveleth would have been
able to expand the payroll to meet the exigencies of
the situation. "If the damn politicians hadn't
grafted so much they could carry some of the people
now like the schools are doing. The schools, you
know, are rich and can carry a lot of people," was
the indictment of a Eveleth merchant.

Virginia, with much less mining tax income,
employed men extensively during this period of depression. The situation is summarized in a statement by a city official:

Our payroll in common labor has jumped from $4,000 per month to $16,000 per month, and still everything is paid for. Every man who is employed by the city is working. We are employing on the average of 600 men per month, two weeks at a time.

Excessive taxation and the squandering of funds has at times been defended by arguments relating to the seasonal nature of mine employment and to the necessity of maintaining the unemployed workers by city "jobs." Politicians have frequently been unscrupulous in stimulating the development of this attitude, and in making the most of it for selfish political gains. Many times the need for city labor has been a subterfuge rather than a reality.

Even "jobs" as a form of relief have produced a mild form of pauperization. It has fostered a spirit of dependence upon public funds. People have developed the attitude that the city and schools owe them a livelihood. Many request work who would never expect or accept outright charity. This imposes an expenditure on the city treasury that probably only a mining community could bear.

Graft: Rumors are current of the widespread practice of graft in the Range towns. The reaction of the voters and juries to exposures of graft indicates that the majority of them have taken it for granted. Everywhere on the Range, as well as outside, one hears of Range graft. The most conclusive evidence is found in the Public Examiner's Reports.

Virginia is not to be included in the discussion of paternalistic and graft mores. This is because there is no tangible evidence of such practice in the city.

Factors in the Development of the Political Mores

Politicians: The politician has played a

dominant role in the towns with a heterogeneous immigrant population. Hibbing and Eveleth each have
such a population, and each have produced leaders
who were master politicians. A mining company official expressed it thus:

> When it comes to being led into politics, these
> foreigners are led into everything by some prominent Amer-
> ican. They are honest, but are easily influenced.

Victor Seabold, president of Hibbing, was no
doubt the most successful politician that ever
raised his head in the Range country. He understood
the common man's psychology. He knew the value of a
slogan, of giving aid to the poor families, of being
interested in humanitarian enterprises, and of playing up the stereotype that was the common object of
hatred--"the Capitalistic Steel Corporation." "The
full dinner-pail" slogan seldom fails to make an appeal to the masses, and especially when this program
is carried out after election. He was the super-man,
idealized by all the immigrant working men. "Vic
said" put a stamp of finality on any issue.

His knowledge of human psychology is also
shown by the fact that he seldom lost a court case
as a lawyer. He could win when everything apparently was against his side of the case.

As a politician Seabold knew how to build
his machine and keep it intact. In order to hold the
business men he threatened to fire any man from the
city payroll who was known to order from a mail-order
house; to hold the workers, all unemployed were put
on the city payroll. His political enemies were
shown to be identified with the mining interests. The
mining interests were the offspring of "eastern capitalists" who were preying on the workers and at the
same time removing the wealth from their community.
Spectacular trials with the mining companies in
which he upheld the injured or those who suffered
property damages, kept him ever in the limelight

Then there were the visits to the legislature to lobby for laws favoring the Range municipalities. At all times the building of great public works for his own Hibbing, consultations with experts and similar activities, kept Seabold and Hibbing before the outside public. Naturally Hibbing could not be thought of without thinking of Seabold.

Victor Seabold has been dead since the year 1926; he lives only in memory now. Yet one cannot broach the subject of politics among Range people in any of the towns without having these memories revived.

Victor Camack, the present mayor of Eveleth, has been in that office for ten years. His praises and curses are far flung throughout the city itself and among the mining officials in adjoining cities. His ability to escape the clutches of the law in the face of accusations and litigation over supposed misuse of city funds testify to his ability to handle the law. Whatever else he may or may not be, he is a skillful politician.

In Virginia one man has acted as city clerk for thirty-seven years. He has kept records that have been above reproach and has doubtless been an important influence in keeping many vicious practices out of government.

Nationality Groups: "The only purpose of Nationality Organizations on the Range is political-- to get jobs." This expresses strongly the place of nationalities in politics. "In Eveleth," says a minister, "people talk of nationalities in terms of votes. There are 250 Italian votes, 300 Austrian votes, 1,000 Slovanian votes, etc."

Great stress is placed on the voting right of the foreign population, and "I'll tell the world they vote." Foreigners covet the privilege of voting, as this is the one road to the "jobs" politicians give in return for the support. Americanization seems to have been given a political cast.

Vocational Insecurity: Vocational insecurity
has given a long arm to the vote, causing the native
born to be no less interested in proper political
affiliations than is the foreigner. "Job consciousness" has been awakened by the scarcity of "jobs."
"There's no work," is the comment of almost every
laborer. The merchants echo the sentiment, for no
work means store bills and poor business. The politicians respond to the situation with made "jobs."
The "job" has been a dominant problem since the 1921
depression. Since 1930 it has been the almost uni-
versal quest on the Range. Public employment has
been the only hope, and this hope is identified with
the right use of political influence and of the bal-
lot. As was suggested by one mother, the wife of a
working man: "Politics is awful. If you say anything you get in bad, and if you don't say anything
you get in bad. It's getting so you can't get any
work unless you're in politics."

Mining companies have also influenced the
vote at times, having urged their employees to vote
for candidates that favored the company's interests.
The mining company affiliation of candidates for office seem to be a major issue in most elections.

The voting interest seems to center basical-
ly about the employment issue. The politician who
can promise the most jobs is likely to carry the election. The vote is the only thing the immigrant has
to sell to the politician for his favors. In case
the mining company is in control of politics, it is
safer to sell the vote there.

Religious Groups: An undercurrent of religious sentiment is reflected in politics. While
candidates do not campaign on the basis of religion,
it is generally known that the religious persuasion
of the candidate, or of his wife, is an influential
factor in either a municipal or school election.

There were seventeen candidates for office
in a recent aldermanic race in Virginia, fifteen

Protestants and two Catholics. A minister express-
ing his sentiments on the outcome of the campaign
said, "The Protestants won, thank God!"
    A man's religion makes a difference in get-
ting votes. In fact, the wife's religion may be a
decided factor with some. "Many Protestants did not
vote for Jones because his wife was a Catholic,"
suggested an Eveleth voter.
    The Ku Klux Klan played an important part in
politics after the World War period. Because of the
secret nature of the operations of this organization, it is difficult to say just what were the consequences of its activities. In Virginia especially, this group fostered an anti-Catholic spirit
that is still felt in both school and municipal
elections. In Hibbing the Klan has about ceased
activities.

    Absentee Ownership: Mining, as the basic
industry, has paid the larger proportion of the taxes
in all the Range towns. The attitude of a politician toward the mining companies is an important
factor in his administration. If he is in sympathy
with the mining interests, it is assumed that he will
be conservative in spending, and will try to foster
a spirit of good will between them and the town. If,
on the other hand, he is directly opposed to the
mining companies, it is assumed that he will get the
most that can be gotten for the people through tax
levies. In each of the towns the mining company and
labor factions have had their "ins" and "outs" in
office.
    Hibbing has had non-mining company presi-
dents almost constantly since 1913. Eveleth has
been in the control of non-company men for several
years. This particular issue in Virginia politics
has been a much less active one because the town has
always been more conservative in its spending.
    Mining towns are abnormal in the sense that
the major taxpayer is not a member of the community

and has little or no control over local government.
In such a setting it is difficult to keep paternalism out of government, and when it once gets in it
is very difficult to eradicate.

The masses have developed a hatred for
"Eastern Capitalists" and for the "Steel Trust."
Just how their stereotypes have been formed one can
scarcely tell. It seems, however, that politicians,
in seeking outside foes upon which to center the attention of the masses in order to escape the scru-
tiny their own behavior has merited, have purposely
created them. The people have generally had a favorable attitude toward the local mining company
superintendents and captains, but they hate the
capitalists "down in New York City and Philadelphia."
The fact that most of the workers for the Oliver
Company are stockholders of the Steel Trust is never
called to their attention. The "Steel Trust" stereotype probably has no counterpart in reality. The
stereotype is none the less real, and the conflict
between the local residents and the Steel Trust is
none the less intense.

Local Traditions: As culture grows in any
area over a period of history the accumulative experiences of the culture building group take on the
nature of cultural compulsives, in that uniformity
in attitudes develops in the common cultural mould.
This similarity in idealogy directs cultural change
toward certain designed ends or in the quest of certain desired values that the group has come to ap-
preciate. On the mental side these compulsives may
be thought of as patterns that have become, through
interaction, the possession of most individuals in
the group. They have continuity in the group and
frequently express themselves in concerted action,
leaving no doubt as to their meaning.

Virginia has fostered a tradition that keeps
it free from paternalistic policy. Public utilities
are municipally owned, but all customers are charged

for them. The installation of public utilities and
monthly rentals are and have been on a purely business basis. The people are satisfied to pay a
reasonable sum for their utilities and to work for
the city, putting in a day at labor, generally speaking.

Victor Seabold introduced the paternalistic
policy into Hibbing government on a wholesale scale.
It carries over to the present time to a great degree. Extravagances in city luxuries are taken as a
matter of course. The "full dinner pail" came to
mean a dinner pail filled by tax moneys.

Camack's mayorship developed a paternalistic
policy in Eveleth. Many soon accepted it as the
order of the day and profited by it when they could
do so. Those traditions acted as compulsives.

Since the enactment of the per capita law,
increasing numbers in Hibbing and Eveleth have become interested in greater municipal thrift, yet the
old drives, resident in individual habit and group
tradition, tend to persist. Thus creating new compulsives is as difficult as is the obliterating of
old ones.

Summary

What then are the factors that have meant
the most in the evolution of the local political
mores? Absentee ownership of taxable resources,
large expenditures to be made by politicians, and
unscrupulous leadership preying upon religious prejudices and immigrant ignorance.

Chapter XIII

LAGS IN GROUP ADJUSTMENT

We have studied in some detail the relationships between the public and the mining companies.
We are primarily concerned in this chapter with the
relationships existing between the laborers and the
mining companies. The gap between the two groups
has widened through the years. The lag in adjustment
between the laborers and the employers is a product
of numerous conflicts that have marked the history of
these groups on the Mesabi. Tardy adjustments of
conflicting issues have intensified antagonism and
thus prepared the way for more bitter conflicts as
new difficulties have appeared. The accumulative effect of these tardy adjustments has been to develop
permanent antagonisms.

Regions of Strain in Mining Company Labor Relations

Basic to an understanding of mining company-
labor relations is the problem of the machine as it
has affected employment.

Mining technology has improved each year,
resulting in fewer jobs and more unemployment.
Practically every improvement in machine technique
has worked a hardship on some group of mine employees. This difficulty has been progressively accumulative. Let us turn to some instances.

The evolution of the machine as it has affected labor can be very clearly seen in the development of open-pit mining methods on the Mesabi.
When the first open-pits were mined, loading was

done with the hand shovel and with chutes built into
the slopes of the pit. The dump cars were crude
affairs, made entirely of wood, with a capacity of
only six or seven tons, and drawn by mules. Then
came the light steam engine, which could draw a
longer train of cars. About 1892, the first steam
shovel was introduced into the Range at Biwabik.
        The electric shovel was introduced about
1923. After a brief trial, it was found so satisfactory that it replaced practically all the steam
shovels. The electric shovels were mounted on
caterpillar wheels so did not require the laying of
track. They had larger dippers, with a five-yard
capacity.
        Of course, similar improvements in technique
have been made in every phase of mining--in handling
ore at the docks, stock piles, and laboratories, as
well as work in the machine shops. Electric loco-
motives have made their appearance, as well as have
automatic switches, doing away with the locomotive
firemen and switchmen. In 1910, the mines were producing 1522 tons of ore for every man employed; in
1920, they produced 2651 tons, and in 1930, 4257
tons.[1]
        While these figures indicate clearly that
more ore is being produced per man, the coming of
more efficient machines made, for a time, more per-
marfent labor conditions. In the early days of open-
pit mining the work was seasonal; as better machines
were developed winter was no obstacle to operations,
so the work of stripping and of piling ore in stock
piles continued through the winter months, even
though the lakes were not open for shipment.
        But this tremendous increase in production
due to modern machinery has made it possible for the
mines to supply the ore demands of the furnaces in a

1. Calculated from figures on men employed and ore produced. See
   Minnesota Mining Directory, and the Annual Reports of the
   St. Louis County Mines Inspector.

very short time. Whereas the mines once had to run
at capacity the entire shipping season, now they
run only a few months to supply the demand. The
large five-yard shovels employed in the last decade
have uncovered enough ore so that very little stripping is necessary. This has brought about the periodic closing of operations for the winter months.

The mine laborer, confronted with the question of present unemployment conditions, invariably
attributes his state to the development of the machine.

It is quite clear from this brief summary of
cultural growth in technology that: First, material
culture has accumulated with great rapidity, the new
and better devices having been added and older machines having been discarded; second, and what is
more important in this connection, adjustments in
group relations have in no way kept pace. The mining companies have been motivated by profits, and
machine technique has been improved at the cost of
the workingman's job. The mining companies have tak-
en the position that the laborer's welfare was not a
matter with which they should concern themselves, or
at least that it was secondary to profits. The laborer has, in turn, become cynical regarding the machine and increasingly hostile in his attitude
toward the mining companies.

A second region of strain has been the issues raised by fanatical labor agitators or by organized labor groups. These issues have led to open
conflict, for each labor strike, if it originates in
and is supported widely by local unions, is the result of the accumulation of unsettled issues between
employer and employee. Let us briefly review the
labor situation on the Mesabi.

Labor organizations as such never have flourished on the Range. Immigrants, unaccustomed to
American ways and unable to speak the American lan-
guage, have constituted a large part of the mining
population. The recent immigrant provided poor material out of which to weld an organization that

could in any way match strength and wits against the
United States Steel and other great corporations
whose subsidiaries mine the ores of the Mesabi. Strike
leaders have been raw immigrants. Americans and An-
glo-Saxon immigrants have held the responsible positions in mining and have had satisfactory incomes, so
they have not been given to labor agitation.

The Range miners have had their conflicts
with employers, notwithstanding. It is perhaps of
little significance that the labor group always lost.
This was to be expected in the nature of things as
they existed on the Range. Labor's struggles were
spasmodic outbursts, often made unwisely. They did
not necessarily grow out of deep felt grievances or
aim at reasonable ends; they were the product of
selfish leaders who, through agitation for selfish
gains, unionized the workers for the period and won
their ends. Not that labor has not had its grievances in mining. They have had them, and in cases
the strike has helped to air them and has indirectly
brought some corrections is working conditions which
have been of far-reaching importance.

There have been three strikes of some conse-
quence on the Mesabi Range.[2] The first was in the
middle nineties, when mining companies had little
use for labor due to the widespread panic throughout
the country; they almost welcomed the strike. At
such a time it could but fail.

The second strike was better timed.[3] The way
had been prepared by a year's sowing of discontent
among workers by members of the Western Federation
of Labor. It broke on July 25, 1907, during the time
of the dock worker's strike at the lake ports. Although the time was opportune for labor to make some
gains, the character of leadership and following

---

2. Each strike is described in detail in Range newspaper files,
   as well as in the historical editions of these papers.
   op. cits.
3. Cheney, C. B., "Labor Crisis and a Governor," Outlook,
   LXXXIX, 24-30

brougnt it to failure. A list of the names of its
leaders is suggestive of their recency in America.
Teofile Petriella (Italian Socialist), H. di Sto-
fane, Oscar Luihlumen, Aate Heiskemon, C. Anderson,
J. Maki, John Kolu, A. Takela, Frank Lucas, John
Movern, R. Lundstrom, E. McHale, F. Menarind, and
J. Connors. These men were representatives of the
Western Federation of Miners, under the general
supervision of Bill Haywood, but as leaders they
failed to inspire the sympathies of the Range communities toward the movement. The merchants refused   credit   to the strikers, and openly con-
fessed their sympathy with the mining companies.

The Finns, with their stubborn determina-
tion, held out to the last. Southern Europeans were
shipped in to replace them. At one time in August
they came 600 strong--Montenegrins, Bulgarians,
Servians, and Greeks.   When the strike was finally
broken, the mining companies refused to employ Finns
who had participated in the Strike. This had far-
reaching consequences to St. Louis County and to the
Range. Thousands of the Finns went into the rural
districts and developed farms. The present state of
development of the hinterland of the Range towns is
largely an outgrowth of this labor crisis.

This exodus of the Finns from the Range
towns and their replacement by Southern Europeans
did much to change the nationality complexion of the
Range, as well as to erect a barrier of animosity
between Finns and the mining companies.

The third and final great struggle of labor
came in 1916, under the leadership of the Interna-
tional Workers of the World. Briefly, the strike
issues were the following: The miners wanted $2.75
per day for open-pit mining, $3.00 per day for un-
derground dry work and $3.50 for underground work.
They wanted an eight-hour day for all, pay twice a
month, and the abolition of the contract system.

The strike leaders of 1907 were the strikers
of 1916, and their sacrifices for the cause of labor

were as futile as were those of the earlier groups.
Workers have been disillusioned regarding
the merits of. unions, and some have lost faith in
the ability of the workers to successfully band together for a common end. Now that hard times have
come, the strike is a useless weapon.

This lack of open resistance, then, does not
indicate amicable relations, so much as it does
hopelessness on the part of labor. Theirs is a pas-
sive resistance that grows out of past failure and a
feeling that the odds are overwhelming, should open
resistance be made. While this is a more peaceful
method than strikes and lockouts, one wonders if
such a state of mind is as healthful as the hope of
gains through staging open and successful resistance.

A third region of strain in labor-industry
relations has centered in the employment issue. No
other issue has been so productive of animosity
toward the mining companies. Idle men brood over
their plight and blame the group that produced it.

Public Sympathy with Labor

The sympathy of the Range public, for the
most part, is with the laboring man. Merchants and
the professions have vested interests in the wages
laborers receive, but the interest probably runs
much deeper. Community prosperity is inevitably
tied up with the prosperity of the working man.

"Business is bad," was the comment of a Virginia grocer in 1932. "Before we had to carry accounts a long time. Now we don't know how long. Bad
before. Worse now."

Community Spending, The Region of Strain
in Public-Mining Company Relations

It has already been clearly indicated by evidence presented in Chapter X that the chief region

of strain in mining company-government relations has
been the matter of public expenditures. Further explanation of the spending pattern in relation to industry is desirable.

The great corporations which replaced most
of the independent companies that took possession of
the Mesabi around 1900 had only one aim--profits
for stockholders. They introduced a predatory pattern in dealing with the employees and with the
State's heritage in ore. The foregoing survey of
the relations between labor and industry suggest
this pattern. The public gradually sided with labor
in their sympathies, and the two groups together,
through controlling government, gradually adopted
the same predatory pattern presented by the mining
companies. Their only weapon was taxation. Through
taxation they could acquire not only poor relief
for labor but subsidies for struggling business enterprises; not only necessary conveniences for the
public good, but luxuries. They found, through taxation, a way to reinstate beauty where industry had
marred it, a way to bring culture and refinement in
a locality where many nations had been mixed in a
struggle for bread, a way to bring recreation and
play to both unemployed youth and adults.

No attempt is made here to justify either
group in this struggle; the aim is simply to try to
explain existing relationships and attitudes.

In fairness to the mining companies it should
be said that many local superintendents have been
men of irreproachable character and of great human
sympathy. It is not these men that laboring groups
and public have hated but the organizations they
have represented. They have liked Fry and Tully,
their local superintendents, but have hated "them
damned capitalists down east." The local representatives were not, however, able to meet the needs
of the local situation because of the system in
which they were enmeshed.

Many humanitarian enterprises have been

developed by the companies, such as the employment
of local social workers to distribute relief, the
establishment of pensions, the beautification of company homes, the provision of a few days work per
month at a time when it would have been more profitable to close the mines entirely, and the provision
in recent years for a mutual welfare committee to
keep in close touch with employees.

In final analysis, it is not a matter of
placing blame; it is a matter of recognizing that a
fundamental lag exists in adjusting relations between industry, labor, and public. Industry is
probably in the best position to take the initiative,
but adjustments in human relations come much harder
than does the development of industrial technology.
The basic maladjustment underlying conflict on the
Range is not unlike that which pervades our industrial civilization.

In conclusion, we may say first, that lags in
certain phases of culture produce and then perpetu-
ate maladjustments in group relations, which group
differences lead to the creation of adaptive culture designed to heal the wounds in group relations.
However, it usually comes so tardily that it does
not completely heal the wounds. Consequently, new
conflict issues break forth calling for further
adoptive culture. In final analysis, group fric-
tions arise over values such as profits and lavish
material culture, which the culture pattern has
created. Group friction leads to the establishment
of adaptive culture through invention or borrowing.
In no case is group friction mitigated completely
by the adaptive culture, for its coming is so long
delayed that animosities tend to control group relations.

P A R T   IV

AN ANALYSIS OF CULTURAL CHANGE

Chapter XIV

THE RÔLE OF THE GREAT MAN IN CULTURAL CHANGE

The fiction, folklore, and drama of the mining town and frontier is vividly colored with characters who dominate the life of the pre-legal period
of settlement. Their influence too carries over into
the early legal period during which the revolver is
more powerful than the law. These dominating characters are powerful men who master by brute force or
by unusual skill or daring with weapons, and masculine women who acquire greatness by violating all
the finer traditions that both men and women in a
more civilized society consider essential to the
female sex. The frontier puts a premium on those
with strong physical powers, who are able to survive the rigors of the natural setting, and those
with elastic moral sense who can tolerate, if not
condone the non-moral order which necessarily exists
when highly civilized men sink to a primitive plane.
    Hardly sufficient evidence exists concerning
characters in the early history of the Mesabi to
make any generalization with regard to the great
men of the period. No one character stands out for
having molded the trend of cultural development or
having exercised the strong arm in social regula-
tion. It was not until the Range became more settled and conflict between mining companies and local
populations began to develop that great men who
wielded a dominant influence stood out in civil affairs.
    During the early period of industrialization
of the Range and soon after the great corporations
had assumed leadership, one man in Hibbing was

influential enough so that it can be said that he
influenced cultural development in a given direction.
Mayor Ray was in office for several years. He was
an Oliver Mining Company sympathizer and therefore
tended to impose the mining company attitudes on the
political structure. He and his councilmen kept the
expenditures of the village low. However, public
improvements were neglected. Board and cinder sidewalks, crowded school houses, and unlighted streets
were symbols of the rigid economy which characterized village life. This pattern led to a violent
reaction during the conflict period.

During the conflict period, also, as we have
seen, one man stands out as a dominant figure, not
only in carrying forward the conflict, but also in
determining the type of cultural development, Victor
Seabold. He defied the mining companies and rallied
to his support the entire citizenry of the Range.
Having done this, he transformed the culture of
Hibbing from that of a primitive mining settlement
to a village with a culture so extravagant that it
rivaled cities five to ten times its size. For ten
years he defied the mining company. With his death
came the end of Hibbing supremacy, and very gradually the mining companies began to assume the position
of dominance which they have since maintained with
increasing effectiveness.

These observations concerning leadership on
the frontier in times of conflict indicate very
clearly that the "great man" is a potent factor in
determining the processes of social changes as well
as in determining cultural trends which characterize
a given period in the history of a community. There
were a number of factors which provided the necessary background in the social and cultural setting
for the triumph of these men as leaders. As far as
social standards were concerned, the communities were
still near the frontier. The unconventional methods
in politics and government which characterize the
frontier were still sanctioned when these men

were elected to official positions. The population
of the community was composed in considerable part
of a foreign element which provided a group that was
readily influenced by the simple promises of the
political leaders. Seabold's greatest success came
while other communities beyond the Range were taking
little interest in the activities of a mining community isolated in the wilderness. Had the activities
of the Mesabi towns in those earlier years been scru-
tinized as carefully by citizens in other parts of
the state and by the state legislature as they are
at the present time, when the state has come to realize the potential revenue that is available through
the iron deposits, it seems hardly likely that he
could have so completely molded the development of
the Range.

During the long conflict period in Range history another character stands in sharp contrast to
the two just described, Alford Ford, city clerk of
Virginia, who kept books conscientiously. He, although playing a less spectacular role, has been
none the less influential. His activities, backed
as they must needs have been by favorable public
sentiment, have been a potent factor in determining
the trend of cultural development. Whether he
could have kept his office in the other two towns
where the citizenry bore considerably less of their
local tax burden is hard to say.

These examples indicate rather clearly one
point. Leaders may play an important part in decid-
ing which interaction process will predominate in a
group at a given time. They also help keep the interaction processes uniform, so that definite interaction patterns are formed and definite trends in
culture building are initiated.

Once an innovator initiates a new interaction process, and a culture trend in a given direction has resulted, both the interaction process and
the culture trend help support the leader's policies
and practices, whether they be of thrift or

extravagance, honesty or graft. This is so much the case that their successors are expected to carry out similar policies. In fact, the attitude of public expectancy enters to enforce the interaction process and the general mores.

Chapter XV

THE LIFE CYCLE OF THE IRON-MINING TOWN

The cyclical change pattern for a total culture postulated by Chapin[1] seems to describe change
in the iron-mining town according to data accumulated herein. Synchronous cycles of change in material and non-material culture are also present as
underlying factors in producing the total picture
of the civilization. However, this analysis of iron
range culture indicates clearly that these synchronous cycles are even more pervasive than indicated
in Chapin's theory; they extend to the realm of
psycho-social, bio-social, and physico-social phenomena as well. Synchronous cycles on these levels,
along with those on the cultural level, produce the
rhythmic rise and fall of the total civilization of
the mining community.

With this brief statement of the hypothesis
let us review a condensed summary of evidence for
rhythmic cycles of change on the levels mentioned.
Let us begin first with the underlying realm of phenomena most remote from culture, the physico-social
and present in order rhythmic changes in bio-social
characteristics, psycho-social characteristics, and
finally present rhythms in culture.

---

1. Cultural Change, ch. 7. See also F. S. Chapin, "A Theory
of Synchronous Culture Cycles," Social Forces, 3, 596-604;
May, 1925. Briefly stated, Chapin's hypothesis is that a
civilization has a life cycle induced by synchronous cycles of material and non-material culture change.

Physico-social Cycles

The first period in the history of the iron range, as far as the present culture is concerned, was occupied with the quest for, and the discovery of, ore. Preliminary investigations indicated the presence of ore, but it took a diligent search by early prospectors to locate ore bodies that could be profitably mined. When profitable bodies were located by the crude hand method, which consisted in sinking a well and windlassing out the refuse, there were the tasks of clearing forests and of building railroads to provide a way to get the ore to markets where it could be sold. The period of discovery and development was possessed of all the risks and uncertainties of a new enterprise. Fortunes that had been made in timber were drowned in ore.[2] In fact, the struggles of the nineties ended with Rockefeller in possession unexpectedly, of a large part of the developed mines and of the first railroad to the district.

Soon after 1900 the range mining enterprise was adequately financed by large corporations with permanent markets. The United States Steel, and other corporations, bought reserves to feed their furnaces for a half century ahead. With the sound financing of the mining enterprises a period of exploitation was ushered in that soon brought shipments above discoveries and hastened the range toward the depletion of high grade ore. In 1915 ore shipments exceeded discoveries as they have at all periods since.[3] The year 1913 marked the maximum remaining tonnage on the range. Since that time ore discoveries have fallen behind shipments about 18,777,000 tons annually.[4] The total shipment of

2. Especially noteworthy is the experience of the seven Merritt brothers who opened the first mines on the Mesabi, and began the building of the first railroad. See P.H. DeKruif, Seven Iron Men.
3. Biennial Report of the Minnesota Tax Commission, 1930, p. 19.
4. Ibid., 1928. Reprint p. 10. This figure includes the Vermilion and Mesabi Ranges together.

ore from the Mesabi mines by decades is as follows:[5]

Period	Mesabi ore shipments tons
1891-1900	31,389,888
1901-1910	193,495,239
1911-1920	332,924,338
1921-1930	331,953,386

The exploitation of ore has been more than exploitation in bulk. The ore of best quality has been taken first. The iron content of ore fell from 56.07 per cent in 1902 to 51.19 per cent in 1929.

In recent years conservation has begun. In fact, it began in earnest about 1920. At that time 35 screening and other "beneficiating" plants had been erected to improve the lower quality ore so that it could be mixed with the good ore and thus prolong the supply. Forty per cent of all ore shipped in 1930 had been "beneficiated."[6] The conservation stage marks the beginning of the end. Eventually the merchantable ores of the Mesabi must disappear and with them the mining towns as such. On May 1, 1930, 43.5 per cent of the merchantable ore had been mined on the Mesabi Range.[7] According to the best estimates the remaining ores will last only 20 to 30 years longer.[8] After that the most that can remain of the prosperous urban civilization of the present

5. Minnesota Mining Directory, 1930.
6. Ibid.
7. Ibid.
8. Eng. and Ming. J. Jl. 17, 1926, p. 84; Ming. and Metalurgy, Aug. 1926, p. 339; Ibid., Jl. 1926, p. 281; Minnesota School of Mines Bul. No. 7.
    It is obvious that no prediction can be absolutely accurate. The future demand for Mesabi ore will be conditioned by the extent to which iron continues to be used in American culture and the degree to which new fields are exploited and their ores imported to the furnace centers by way of the St. Lawrence. The future of the range will also depend upon the degree to which low grade ores can be utilized at a profit, which in turn depends upon tax rates in Minnesota, transportation costs, mining costs, "beneficiating" costs, etc.

mining communities is small rural trade centers with
meagre agricultural hinterlands.

Summarizing briefly, the physico-social cycles on the Mesabi have been first, a period of
quest for and discovery of an unknown resource which
spent most of its force by 1915; second, a period
of wasteful exploitation of a resource that seemed
inexhaustible that reached its climax just preceding 1920; third, a period of conservation of a rapidly diminishing resource which began in earnest
about 1920 but which has probably not yet reached
its climax. The period of serious decline in ore
may be delayed for some little time, but the ore
will, according to best estimates, be exhausted in
approximately 20 or 30 years, thus marking the end
of the mining civilization.

These fluctuations are represented graphi-
cally in the lower part of Figure II. The time span
is represented on the base line and the intensity
of the cycle on the vertical, the peak of the curve
representing the time of its greatest intensity. The
dates of the beginning and end of the cycles are
only approximate since the phenomena described are
of a historical nature and, therefore, are not
abrupt. They are, nevertheless, periodic and can be
represented approximately.

Bio-social Cycles

The mining town is characteristically a
boom town in its youth. A rapid growth to maturity,
a period of relatively stable population numbers,
and then a rapid decline characterize the three
population growth cycles. The period of boom growth
with the Mesabi towns ended soon after 1905. Previous to this time the population increased one hundred to three hundred per cent each five year period.
(See Table I.) Virginia in 1900 was an exception,
which is explained by a fire in that year which

Table I

Population of the Three Range Towns Showing
Percentage Increase for Census Periods, 1895-1930*

Year	Hibbing		Virginia		Eveleth	
	Total Number	Per Cent Increase	Total Number	Per Cent Increase	Total Number	Per Cent Increase
1895	1,085		3,647		764	
1900	2,481	128.7	2,962	-18.8	2,752	260.2
1905	6,566	164.7	6,056	104.5	5,332	93.8
1910	8,832	34.5	10,473	72.9	7,936	32.0
1920	15,089	70.8	14,022	33.9	7,205	2.4
1930	15,666	3.8	11,963	-14.7	7,484	3.9

*Source: 1895 and 1905, State Census. Other years Federal
Census, as the State Census was discontinued in 1905.

destroyed a large part of the town. The towns made
a good growth up to 1920, but since that time have
remained practically stationary in population. Virginia declined approximately 15 per cent in population during the decade 1920-1930.

The mining town during its frontier stage is
masculine in the extreme. The census, taken the
third year after the founding of Virginia and the
second year after the settlement of Hibbing and
Eveleth, indicates that the ratio of males to females in Eveleth was six to one, in Hibbing five to
one, and in Virginia three to one. From this extreme
the trend has been gradually toward a balanced ratio.
The 1930 census indicates that the sexes have about
reached a balance. The number of males per 100 females for each census period was as follows:

Sex Ratio of the Three Iron Range Towns, 1895-1930

Year	1895	1905	1910	1920	1930
Hibbing	474.1	201.9	*	149.9	105.0
Virginia	271.0	190.1	169	118.5	103.4
Eveleth	600.9	177.6	*	*	107.1

The mining town is, in the beginning, a town of adults, probably consisting chiefly of young men between the ages of 20 and 40, venturesome in temperament, full of vitality and courage. Weaklings cannot survive the primitive conditions of life that must be endured during the prospecting and development period. No statistical data on age groups of the Mesabi towns are available for the first eighteen years of their history, but the opinion given is in the main correct. The second period in the history of the mining town is characterized by a youthful population. Young people with families move in and produce offspring at a high rate. On the Mesabi these groups were largely foreign, as has been true doubtless in most American mining towns. This high birth rate leads to a relatively large number in the lower age group, as is clearly indicated in Figure I which shows the relative percentage of school pupils in the various grades.[9] For the years 1895 to 1920 the primary group was abnormally large in the school population. At the same time the advanced pupils were relatively scarce.[10] As the population has aged and the birth rate has fallen, population in the primary grades has fallen markedly, and in 1930 a decreasing proportion in the intermediate grades is noted, whereas the

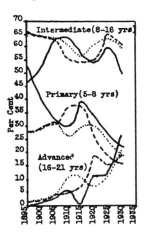

Fig. 1. Trends in School Population in Three Mesabi Iron-Range Towns, 1895-1930.
Key:——Hibbing;----Eveleth;·····
     ...... Virginia

9. School data are used since the towns were too small to be analyzed into age groups in the U. S. Census in the early periods.
10. This trend is offset in part by changed educational mores for the upper age group, the building of local junior colleges, etc.

higher grades were then most completely filled with
pupils. The final "age group" cycle in the mining
towns will be characterized by an abnormally large
adult population. Declining industry will cause
youth to leave for fields of opportunity elsewhere.
The old will remain behind with vested interests in
the community. The Mesabi has not reached this
stage fully as yet, but the relative number in the
upper age groups as compared to the lower age groups
has changed markedly in the last ten years as indicated in Table II. The group above 45 years of age
was abnormally low in 1920 compared to the state,
but in 1930 it was practically normal. The group
under five years was low in 1930 compared to the
state, and the group under 20 years of age was also
low. The group 20 to 44 years was still high but
not nearly as high as in 1920. These trends indicate that the range will soon have an abnormally
large population in the upper age groups.

During the first period of the mining town's
history births are few because of the disproportion
of the sexes, and the sparsity of married couples.
This period ends with the coming of prolific and
youthful immigrant stocks which produces a high birth
rate. Data on this point are incomplete but such as
exist justify this summary statement. Hibbing's
birth rate was about 45 per thousand for the period
1900 to 1909,[11] approximately 30 per thousand from
1920 to 1924, and about 22 per thousand from 1925 to
1929.[12] For the years 1928 and 1929 the rate was 20
which is about normal as compared to the United
States registration area.[13] The rate for Virginia

---

11. Table XVII, Third Biennial Report, Minn. State Board of
    Health, 1911.
12. Unpublished tabulations in the office of the State Board
    of Health in St. Paul. Available only for the years
    cited.
13. Annual Reports United States Census, Births, Stillbirths
    and Infant Mortality Statistics.

was very low for the first four years following the
fire of 1900, but from 1905 to 1909 and 1915 to 1920
(data are not available for intervening years) was
considerably above that of the United States registration area. Since 1920, Virginia's birth rate
has fallen below the registration area. In 1929 it
was only 15.6 per 1000.[14]

Table II

Percentage of Population in Various Age Groups for Hibbing
and Virginia Compared to the State of Minnesota, 1920 & 1930*

Age	Hibbing		Virginia		Minnesota	
	1920	1930	1920	1930	1920	1930
years						
Under 20	43.5	42.4	38.0	40.2	40.4	44.5
Under 5	13.0	8.9	11.8	7.3	11.0	10.4
20 to 44	43.5	38.8	48.6	38.0	38.8	33.7
45 and above	13.0	18.9	13.4	21.7	20.8	21.8

* Eveleth is omitted as it is under 10,000 population and,
 therefore, population is not analyzed for age groups in the
 U. S. Census.

        The fluctuations in the death rate cannot be
studied on the Mesabi because of a lack of complete
data. Figures, available for Virginia for the years
1910 to 1927, and for Hibbing from 1918 to 1927, indicate that the rate has been considerably lower
than for the United States registration area. This
has been especially true since 1920 when deaths have
been about eight per thousand in the range towns as
compared to about 13 or 14 in the United States registration area.[15] Newspaper accounts make clear
that the infant death rate was excessively high on
the range during the two decades 1900 to 1920.

14. Op. cit.
15. Mortality Statistics, U. S. Census.

Violent deaths have also been high due to industrial hazards. Beyond this we can make no comments.

The bio-social cycles discussed are summarized in the next to the bottom part of Figure II. In this case the composite cycles in the three towns are illustrated, each line representing the origin, climax, and disappearance of the combined bio-social cycle of the three range towns.

Psycho-social Cycles

The matter of group attitudes over a period of history cannot well be measured statistically, yet newspaper accounts, and other local records, current group opinions readily expressed in interviews, as well as certain group activities, indicate quite as clearly the prevailing inter-group attitudes of a community. On the basis of such evidence the conclusions summarized below were reached, and are presented here without proof because of a lack of space.[16]

The first period was one of community integration. Laborers, industrialists, and public (groups represented in local government) in the range communities worked together in the face of common dangers and common hazards to maintain themselves and found their civilization. Forest fires,[17] severe winters, uncertainties in finding a market for the ore, and other similar circumstances kept the community integrated to an unusual degree. Soon after 1900, when the great corporations took over the mines, and when the towns were well founded an

16. See full ms. for a complete summary of historical events.
17. Virginia was completely destroyed by a forest fire in 1893 and a large part of the business section was again destroyed in 1900 by a fire originating in a local sawmill. All of the range towns were threatened again and again by forest fires.

Explanation of Figure II

The figure at the top in the form of a normal curve represents the growth, maturity and decline of the mining town civilization. The first period is the pioneer period which represents what Chapin has called the period of growth; the middle period of the mining civilization is one of conflict, which corresponds to Chapin's period of maturity; the final period on the Mesabi will be one of decay and disintegration. The mining towns will no doubt eventually be replaced by small agricultural trade centers.

The diagrams on the four levels below represent minor cycles of change. Each minor cycle is described as follows:

Culture Cycles

—— Life Evaluation Cycles (Mores)
 1. Life held cheap
 2 and 3. Well-developed protective culture
----------Moral Standards Cycles (Mores)
 1. Tolerance of vice
 2. Tolerance of paternalism
  and graft
 3. Economy mores in government
--------Material Culture Cycles
 1. Simple material culture
 2. Lavish material culture
 3. Decay of material culture

Psycho-social Cycles

—— Group Relations Cycles
 1. Integration
 2 and 3. Conflict
-------Dominance and Submission
 Cycles
 1. Public ascendancy
 2. Mining Company ascendancy
-------Industrial Groups Cycles
 1. Individual capitalists
 2 and 3. Predatory corporations

Bio-social Cycles

—— Birth Rate Cycles
 1. Few married couple and few
  births
 2. High birth rate
 3. Low birth rate
----- Age Groups Cycles
 1. Young adult males
 2. Disproportionately large
  number of children
 3. Disproportionately large
  number of old people
------- Population Growth Cycles
 1. Boom growth
 2. Stable population
 3. Decline
------Sex Ratio Cycles
 1 and 2. Males predominant
 3. Balanced

Physico-social Cycles

—— Geographical Resource Cycles
 1. Extent of ore unknown
 2. Abundant supply located
 3. Supplying rapidly diminishing
------ Social Policy Cycles
 1. Discovery and development
 2. Exploitation
 3. Conservation

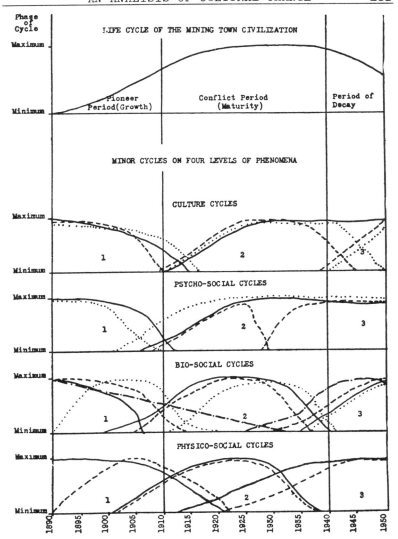

Fig. II. A Superimposition of Change Cycles on the Physio-Social, Bio-social, Psycho-social and Cultural Levels Indicating Their Synchronization on the Mesabi Iron Range.

inter-group conflict cycle developed that reached
its climax in about 1912 and continues unabated.
This period ushered in periodic industrial conflicts,
and more important still, perpetual public-mining
company conflict. Mining company taxes were the
chief issue of contention. The towns began a regime
of spending that led the mining companies to insti-
tute lawsuits and various restraining actions against
them and their building and recreation programs.
Allegations of graft in public office became the order of the day in city government.[18] Politicians
made the most of their office to reward their friends;
patronage existed on every hand. The predatory pattern of the heartless and exploiting corporations
became that of the local community also, and the mining companies were the victims of it. Besides paying
large tax revenues the companies faced many damage
suits in Hibbing which aimed at collecting damages
for blasting near residences and at receiving remun-
eration for the deterioration of property values due
to mining activities.

Each group has carried its issues into the
state courts and into the state legislatures. Citizens' damage suits against the companies have been
carried to the United States Supreme Court. Each
group has tried to gain at the expense of the other.
Up to 1920 the towns held the position of ascendancy
and defied the mining companies successfully, but
always with a narrow margin of power. Since that
time the tide has turned and the mining companies
are making the communities bow. The original death
blow to town domination came in the per capita tax
limitation law of 1921 which limited expenditures
for municipal purposes to $100 per person. The law
was amended in 1929 calling for further reductions
annually until 1933 and thereafter when expenditures are limited to $70 per capita. There is

18. This is not true of Virginia, probably due in part to the
    relatively larger part of taxes paid by local residents
    as compared to Hibbing and Eveleth.

considerable evidence that hereafter the mining companies will dictate local policies to a much greater
degree.

The group factor and the dominant inter-group
attitudes can be presented diagrammatically in a
similar chart to the foregoing indicating dates when
the characteristic psycho-social phenomena were most
characteristic, so are summarized in the middle section of Figure II.

Cultural Cycles

The mores. The municipal mores of the mining
town experience three distinct phases. First there
is a period of tolerance of vice prostitution, gambling, fighting, and drinking. This is clearly indicated in the papers of the nineties in the Mesabi
towns. Numerous accounts of drunken brawls, deaths
from exposure of homeless men in drunken stupors,
stabbing affrays, reports of the capture of escaped
criminals who had fled from other cities to the range
towns to lose their identity, raids on gambling devices by county officials, cases of the passing of
counterfeit money, of the printing and forging of
mining company and lumber company checks, of the
jumping of rooming-house board bills and of hotel
bills, of the operating of "blind pigs" to avoid the
payment of the liquor license--all these appear as
news items. According to statements of early residents, prostitutes, gamblers, and saloon keepers had
a respectable status in the communities. The prostitute walked the streets by day without shame or
disgrace and the saloon keeper's favor was to be
courted if one were in politics.

Before 1910 the purity leagues succeeded in
changing the more on these points and the house of
prostitution sought the wilderness outside the towns
or disappeared; the saloons were regulated by state
laws, and the gamblers plied their trade in secret

or moved on to new frontiers.

Public mores from 1910 to 1930 can best be
characterized by the general concept of patronage
plus many extravagances in public spending; these
were not only practiced but sanctioned by community
mores. The patronage cycle is a phase of the conflict pattern--the local communities have fought the
predatory corporations through preying upon tax revenues. The mores have sanctioned the predatory pattern as it is exercised by the communities. The
people say, "Let's get all we can. If we don't get
it, it will go to buy cigars for them damn capitalists down East."

As ore reserves decline undoubtedly the
municipal mores will come to be characterized by
economy to some degree. Perhaps this characteristic
of the mores will lag far behind the need for it. At
least this has been the case in Hibbing and Eveleth
since the enactment of the per capita limitation law.
Expenditures in Eveleth have each year run over the
per capita limit, and injunctions against spending
more have been imposed by the mining companies. Her
obligations are about a year ahead of her income. The
need exists for economy mores and some of the citizens want economy. Many of them, however, still want
the spoils of political patronage.

Another field of the mores quite definitely
marked is that involving the regard for life, or what
might be termed the "protective complex" of the society. During the early days in the mining towns,
life was cheap, partly from carelessness, partly from
necessity. Natural catastrophe took a toll here
where the sheltering influence of well-developed material culture did not exist; vice also took a high
toll here where the mores did not protect a man
against his lower appetites; suicide took a toll here
where single men were detached from family and
friends; industry took a toll, for basic needs called
for practical rather than protective machinery. Naturally life came to be held cheap.

The suicide rate since 1900 is shown in Table
III. Up to 1910 it was excessively high. It was
probably much higher than these figures indicate as
the State of Minnesota did not get into the United
States registration area until that time. The cards
reporting deaths indicate that a death was violent
but frequently fail to indicate whether it was accidental, suicidal, or homicidal. The absence of suicide cases in Eveleth from 1901-1905 is probably due
to poor reporting, for there were violent deaths during the period for which the method of commission is
not indicated.

The fatality rate in the St. Louis County
mines per 1000 workmen has been as follows:[19]

Period	Fatalities per 1000
1898-1905	5.93
1906-1910	4.82
1911-1915	2.64
1916-1920	2.52
1921-1925	2.05
1926-1930	1.81

Material culture cycles. Definite cycles in
material culture can be observed and measured as
well. The financial index is probably the most in-
dicative of the state of material culture of a community. For the sake of brevity the per capita total
tax levied in the three towns for all purposes
(Table IV) and the per pupil value of all schoolhouses and sites (Table V) only are presented here.
Each set of figures tells the same story,--a period
of simple, crude material culture which ended before
1910, followed by a rapid flowering of material culture which probably reached its climax around 1930
(considering the existence of the per capita law).
Soon decline will come with decreased revenues.

19. Annual Report, St. Louis County Mine Inspector, 1905 to
1930. For previous years see Biennial Reports of Minnesota
Department of Labor. Most of the Mesabi Range is located
in St. Louis County.

Table III

Number of Suicides and Rates per 100,000 Summarized by Five-
Year Periods for the Three Range Towns* and for the
United States Registration Area **

Period	Hibbing		Eveleth		Virginia		U.S. Registration Area
	No.	Rate	No.	Rate	No.	Rate	Rate
1901–1905	7	28.4	0	0	15	73.1***	13.9
1906–1910	11	27.8	7	22.0	6	13.8	16.0
1911–1915	5	9.3	5	14.1	11	19.1	16.3
1916–1920	3	4.3	1	2.8	8	12.0	12.3
1921–1925	9	11.8	6	16.5	12	17.9	12.1
1926–1930	14	18.0	9	24.2	15	23.9	13.2#
1901–1930	49	14.4	28	14.2	67	21.1	14.0

*Data for Range towns were tabulated from the card files of
the State Board of Health, St. Paul
**United States rate is an average of annual rates. The av-
erage for Range towns is an actual average of periods as
given based on estimated aggregate population and aggregate suicides for the respective periods.
***For 1902–1905 only. No records were kept for 1901. The
fire probably led in part to the high rate.
#1926–1928 only.

Cycles in material culture and in the mores
are summarized diagrammatically in that part of Figure II labeled "culture cycles."

Summary

In the foregoing pages certain selected cycles have been presented to indicate the synchronous
nature of periodic cycles on four levels of phenomena in the mining town.

In the study of the Range it early became obvious that there have been two rather distinct periods in its history. The pioneer period is clearly
marked by certain definite characteristics. Gradually this shifted to a period of extravagance which

Table IV

Per Pupil Value of Schoolhouses and Sites
1895-1930*

Year	Hibbing	Virginia	Eveleth
1905	$ 57.07	$ 97.94	$111.10
1910	177.67	15.77	113.13
1920	119.63	188.49	144.68
1925	603.40	395.87	257.35
1930	707.95	727.88	431.15

* Based on County Superintendent's annual reports to the State
Superintendent of Public Instructions. All values are reduced to the 1910-1914 dollar values on the basis of the
wholesale price index developed by the U. S. Department of
Labor. Data are not available for 1915.

has persisted to the present time. During very recent years evidence of decline is beginning to be
observed, and certain tendencies indicate that soon
there will be a marked decline. The pioneer period
ended between 1905 and 1910. This was followed by
the period of extravagance. The period of decay began only recently and decay may not become characteristic for ten or fifteen years yet.

In order to make Figure II complete, then,
this life cycle has been presented in the form of a
growth curve similar to that in Chapin's theoretical
graph, and this curve has been superimposed on the
time chart along with the diagrams representing minor
cycles of change.

Table V

Per Capita Total Taxes Levied, 1900-1930*

Year	Hibbing	Virginia	Eveleth
1900	$ 8.54	$ 2.87	$ 1.66
1905	22.72	2.65	10.74
1910	86.24	47.32	38.68
1915**	137.78	50.03	69.82
1920	134.73	48.30	121.61
1925	209.00	68.49	140.10
1930	219.64	92.05	173.40

* Based on State Auditor's Annual Reports. All values are reduced to the 1910-1914 dollar values on the basis of the
  wholesale price index developed by the U. S. Department of
  Labor.
** Figures approximate rather than exact as populations for
  these years are estimated.

The composite figure indicates that certain
synchronous cycles mark fairly definitely the pioneer
period of the mining town (Chapin's period of integration), other cycles mark the period of maturity,
and certain trends that are now in the making indicate that still others will characterize the final
period. The three historical phases of the life cycle are broken by the shifting minor cycles as nearly as historical trends are ever broken. Naturally
the old gradually merges into the new. The dating
of any historical event is to some extent arbitrary.
The general period of origin and decline of a cycle
can, nevertheless, be observed.

Synchronization does not necessarily mean
causation. It may only indicate coincidence. However, if one examines the nature of the cycles on
the various levels it becomes obvious that there is
a causal relation between the cycles on the four
levels and the total municipal civilization. The

characteristic civilization proves to be a composite
of these influences as can be induced from the preceding discussion, and as might be much further
elaborated if space permitted. There is an interrelation between the minor cycles on the different
levels also. For instance, the social policy of exploitation grows out of the fact of the apparent in-
exhaustibleness of ore; the poorly developed protective mores are due to the emergencies of the frontier and to the predominance of the male sex in the
population; the vice mores grow out of the uneven
sex ratio also. Social integration is produced by
the mutual struggle for maintenance which in turn is
explained in part by the individual (rather than
corporate as in the later period) nature of the mining enterprise.

The concurrent disappearance of a series of
minor cycles and the initiation of new ones marks
the beginning and end of periods in the total civilization of the mining towns. The period of maturity
is not primarily a matter of a massing of a majority
of cycles as suggested in Chapin's discussion, but
in this case appears to be the product of minor cycles most of which are peculiar to the period. This
superimposition suggests another interesting characteristic. Minor cycles in those realms most remote
from culture change first, while changes in culture
itself lags behind. Change in the resource aspects
for instance foreshadows an ultimate change in culture building trends. The change in the resource
may not be reflected in culture until some years after it is obvious in the lower level. Abundance of
ore followed by corporate management, followed by a
public-mining company conflict will be followed by
extravagance in culture. A period of delay between
the appearance of the socio-geographical factor and
its reflection in culture building seems natural
when one stops to analyze it in a community which
is so closely dependent upon a single resource.

By way of caution it should be stated that in
this discussion no attempt has been made to analyze

the influence of outside contemporary culture in
stimulating or directing the changes that have occurred on the Mesabi. It must, of course, be recognized that underlying the exploitation of the ores
of the Mesabi lay the demands of an iron age in the
larger world outside. Likewise the machine culture
dominating range civilization is a part of the American complex as are all phases of the culture. The
problem has not been to emphasize this aspect, but
rather to show how contemporary American culture as
represented in the rather unique configuration of an
iron range passes through its life cycle as a unique
type of civilization.

The validity of Chapin's hypothesis is at-
tested by the culture of the mining town, and it is
clear that the periodic synchronous minor cycles not
only characterize material and non-material culture,
but also underlying levels of phenomena bearing directly upon cultural change in a given area.

Whether the life cycle theory is applicable
to cultures universally is beyond the scope of this
discussion. If it is applicable to cultures in general[20] one striking difference from the mining town
cycle would probably be found. The time span of
the culture would be much greater. The transitory
nature of the mining town is too well known to justify proof. The mining town appears with the discovery and demand for the resource its area possesses. When the resource is gone it vanishes, leaving
behind only the ghostlike shadow of its former prosperity. A civilization built on a soil resource,
which is exhausted very slowly, might well have a
life cycle spanning centuries.

---

20. Wissler suggests, "Tribal cultures have life cycles, like
individuals of a species. They spring from parent cultures, grow, mature, beget other cultures, decline, and
eventually die." Man and Culture, p. 212.

Chapter XVI

WHERE DOES THE DYNAMICS OF CULTURAL CHANGE RESIDE?

Cultural Change and Social Change
as Distinct Processes

Studies in social or cultural change have so
far not differentiated social and cultural change.
In fact, the tendency seems to have been to consider
social change and cultural change terms that may be
used interchangeably. For the purpose of some studies a distinction may not be necessary since the
social and cultural are vitally related. When one
comes to locate the drive back of cultural change,
however, a clear definition of these realms of phenomena seems desirable.

The social and the cultural are in reality
distinct phenomena. Society is composed of interacting groups of individuals, whereas culture is composed of tools, methods, codes, and forms that the
interacting groups produce and through which they
function. A similar distinction may be made in dis-
cussing change. Social change would then be used
to describe changes in society, and cultural change
to describe changes in culture.

In this discussion, therefore, "cultural
change" will be confined strictly to changes in the
man-made tools, mores, and folkways. "Social
change" will be used to describe changes in group
composition (age, sex, vitality, mobility, etc.) **and**
changes in the interaction processes (conflict; cooperation, domination, subordination, etc.) that
characterize inter- and intra-group relations.

The distinction between the social and the
cultural is recommended, especially in studies of
social and cultural change in order that we may
avoid the common error of attributing to culture
forces which it does not possess. The use of such
phrases as "culture is dynamic," "culture produces
culture," "history repeats itself," unless they are
carefully defined erroneously implies that culture
has resident forces which in reality reside in the
social group and not in culture. There may be no
objection to the use of such phrases as long as they
are confined to a purely descriptive meaning imply-
ing only that culture does change and is not, therefore, perpetually the same. They can, however, hardly be accepted when held to mean that there are forces resident in culture which produce change in culture. On the other hand, there seems to be no comparable objection to saying that "the group produces
culture," "society is dynamic," "group experience
determines culture trends."

An exact definition of cultural change and
social change will differentiate them and in so doing will clear the ground for a more penetrating
analysis of both social change and cultural change.

In this study of cultural changes in the
mining towns on the Mesabi Iron Range in Minnesota
it became apparent that the fundamental forces directing cultural change and shaping the culture pattern existed outside of culture although they were
intimately related to it. They were for the most
part social forces as above defined.

Relations of Group Interaction Pattern
to the Culture Pattern

The pioneer period in the history of the
mining towns was distinguished from later periods by
definite social characteristics such as a predomi-
nantly large male population, a disproportionately

large prostitute class of women, a disproportionately large age group in the most energetic period of
life. The mines were privately owned and were operated on a small amount of capital. Although everyone on the range depended upon the mines for a living, their success was uncertain. This situation
produced a high degree of integration in the mining
town society. Cooperation was necessary in order to
assure maintenance and survival of the social group
in the struggle with nature.

As soon as survival was assured, a more normal population group migrated to the area--women and
children, married men, and business and professional
classes. Great corporations, including the United
States Steel Corporation, purchased the ore reserves.
This constituted a change in the composition of the
social groups. A change in the interaction pattern
accompanied this change. Absentee ownership of the
iron mines by corporations initiated an era of
strikes on the part of the laboring group and of lawsuits between mining companies and the range towns.
The societal interaction pattern thus became a conflict pattern.

It is these changes that have been designated "social changes," changes in group composition
and in the dominant interaction patterns of the society. The term "culture change" is not at all applicable to them, although culture change proceeds
along with these social changes and may be to a
considerable extent induced by them.

Culture, on the other hand, during the pioneer period was very primitive. Folkways were realistic, and the mores tolerated many forms of behavior condemned in normal American communities.
Mesabi Range pioneers lived near to nature, wresting
a food supply largely from the native animal life
and making shelters from logs and rough unplaned
lumber taken from the native pine trees. The saloon
keeper, the gambler, the prostitute, the escaped
criminal and renegade from established towns beyond

were all accepted as satisfactory citizens. Numbers
were more important than quality in these communities where forest fires, severe winters, and hard
work called for courage and endurance rather than
refinement.

As the society became more normal in group
composition, culture changed very markedly. Complete
families in the towns soon reduced the prostitute to
a shameful status; the gambler had to learn to ply
his trade in secret or move on to a new frontier;
the saloon keeper was forced to abide by the state
law on closing hours. The coming of professional
people, of conservative business men, along with the
increase in complete families and children soon led
to the abandonment of board sidewalks, muddy streets,
mining shacks, and cheap frame school buildings and
put in their place public works unrivaled by American
communities of equal size. These changes in the
mores and folkways and in the material culture of the
towns have been called cultural changes.

Culture Change as the Product of Interaction

When social change and cultural change are
differentiated it becomes obvious that the two
processes are to be a considerable degree causally
connected. The data accumulated in this study of
mining towns indicate that social change is in most
cases the forerunner of cultural change and frequently induces the cultural change. This may be illustrated by showing how the change in the culture pattern of the mining towns seem to have been brought
about by a change in the dominant intergroup interaction pattern characterizing the society in two
periods of its history.

During the pioneer period when integration
characterized relations between the public, the mining companies and labor, the municipal culture pattern was marked by thrift, conservatism, economy,
and simplicity. In the later period when the public

and labor took a conflict attitude toward the mining
companies, the municipal culture pattern became predatory in nature. Enormous sums of money were spent
for public works, athletic programs and recreation.

The social interaction pattern characterized
by group integration and solidarity of the first
period was causally connected in the case cited with
the thrift pattern in municipal culture. When life
for all groups was a struggle and when success was
uncertain the matter of economy was of common in er-
est to the public, the laborer, and the industrial-
ist. Likewise in the second period there was a causal connection between the conflict of groups and
extravagance in municipal culture. Extravagance in
expenditure for public ornaments and public works
was an expression of conflict between local residents and absentee corporation taxpayers. Thus in a
very direct way change in the intergroup relation
(a social change) predicated a definite change in
the municipal culture pattern.

While a direct and causal connection between
change in a social interaction pattern and a culture
pattern exists, the analysis here has been oversim-
plified. To make it more complete it must be pushed
back to lower levels of phenomena in the community.

The problem of change as it affects culture
may be attacked at four rather distinct levels. The
first level, that of changes in the physical environment, is basic, although as such it is quite far
removed from cultural change. The physical environment undergoes two distinct types of change from the
viewpoint of causation. The one consists in those
changes that are initiated by forces inherent in
nature. These changes, with the exception of cata-
clysmic changes, are orderly and recurrent, such as
climatic and seasonal changes. Culture is to a considerable degree adjusted to these changes and tends
to conform to them from season to season. These adjustments come so automatically that they are seldom
thought of as initiating forces in cultural change.

On the frontier, however, men have to reckon with them in making initial adjustments. The other type of change in the natural environment is much more direct and consequential to cultural change. It consists of those changes that grow out of human activity in the environment. Such activities as improving natural surroundings, harnessing natural sources of power, discovering and using natural resources, all of which grow out of man's progressive adjustments to the natural setting, are typical of these changes.

Among the changes wrought in the physical environment by human activity on the Mesabi Iron Range have been the exhaustion of forests, the partial exhaustion of high-grade ores, the partial depletion of wild life, the clearing of lands and establishment of farms. These changes have reflected on societal activity and culture in many ways and have thus become determinants of other societal activities in the area. In this sense the tightening of the state industrial policy in relation to taxes and profits, the psychological outlook of labor as refers to security, tenure of position, and opportunity for work, the prospects of trade for business enterprises, these, and many similar changes may all be traced to diminishing resources in the natural environment wrought by the human impact upon it.

The second general level of change that bears on cultural change is the biological, that of changing population quality and numbers as these factors influence culture. This problem involves the question of relative mental capacity of different groups in the society, the problem of the sex ratio, and to some extent the distribution of social classes, and the density of population. Presumably all of these factors bear on cultural change, along with other variant characteristics of the human stock.

On the Mesabi Range, nationality groups have changed with the different waves of immigrants.

Because of different experiences and capacities for adjustment, these peoples have played varying roles in the range communities. Nationality groups must be taken into account in interpreting birth and death rates, and also such cultural characteristics as are exhibited in fraternal, political, religious, and educational institutions.

Male-female ratio in the population, as well as other phases of the selective migration to the range during the period of its settlement was shown to have been important in shaping certain phases of the culture. Especially did the uneven sex ratio affect sex mores.

Changes in group composition and interaction constitute the third level of change. This aspect of change is exclusively in the social and sociological realm. Here is located the dynamic element in all cultural change, and the dynamic element for the second type of geographical change described, that of change in the environment through the agency of man, and also the force producing many of the changes just described.

Whether labor or capital, Protestant or Catholic, Democrat or Republican, industrial group or public plays the dominant rôle makes a difference in culture building. As control on the Mesabi Range shifted from one group to another, social organization was modified, and new cultural trends were initiated. The relationships existing between the groups in society started currents of interaction that had far-reaching import. Long prevailing interaction patterns in the group furnished the drive for consistent and long prevailing trends in culture building, as has been suggested in the preceding section.

It must be recognized that culture history is important to cultural change, as well as to geographical, biological, and social change. There is an intimate interrelation between all of these aspects of change. The natural and cultural environments are the _milieu_ in which social interaction

takes place. If man exhausts the soil or wastes the
timber or ore, group interaction ceases because man
abandons the area; if man modifies his customs,
changes his laws, or perfects his tools, social interaction is modified by greater restrictions or
greater freedom. Moreover, the cultural background
provides the standards of value and the tools for
the struggle for resources, and the culture defines
the pattern for the struggle and sets its limits.
With regard to selective migration to an area it may
be said that the culture provides the standards of
value which make certain resources of nature act as
magnets drawing only certain population elements.
The social group is the agent initiating change in
the four realms described--geography, human biology,
society, and culture--granting the exceptions noted.[1]
Culture, like natural resources, and human capacity
provide the conditions for social interaction.

---

1. Changes in geography and biology that are wholly natural, and
   beyond human control.